The Political Economy
of
Health Care Reforms

Huizhong Zhou
Editor

2001

W.E. Upjohn Institute for Employment Research
Kalamazoo, Michigan

The facts presented in this study and the observations and viewpoints expressed are the sole responsibility of the authors. They do not necessarily represent positions of the W.E. Upjohn Institute for Employment Research.

Cover design by J.R. Underhill.
Index prepared by Diane Worden.
Printed in the United States of America.

The Political Economy
of
Health Care Reforms

Contents

Acknowledgments

The chapters in this volume are based on lectures presented at the thirty-sixth Annual Public Lecture-Seminar Series in the 1999–2000 academic year. The series was conducted by the Department of Economics at Western Michigan University and was made possible through generous financial support from the W.E. Upjohn Institute for Employment Research and the College of Arts and Sciences of Western Michigan University. I wish to express my gratitude to my colleagues in the Department of Economics for their support and encouragement, especially the members of the Lecture-Seminar Series Committee, Professors Donald Alexander and Bassam Harik of the Department of Economics, and Dr. Allan Hunt of the W.E. Upjohn Institute for Employment Research.

Introduction

Huizhong Zhou
Western Michigan University

Health care is an important component of an economy that involves the provision of goods and services by both the private and public sectors, economic and other regulations, and public policies. As health care technologies have advanced rapidly in the past few decades and the demand for health care continues to grow, health care expenditures have been increasing steadily in industrialized nations. In the United States, for example, health care expenditures as a share of the gross national product (GNP) grew from 7.4 percent in 1970 to 9.3 percent in 1980, and to 12.4 percent in 1990. It reached more than 15 percent of the GNP in 1995. Changes in the health care supply and demand have prompted changes in health care finance, insurance, and service delivery. Health care reforms have become an ever-present subject in federal as well as state politics for the past decade. Although there have been no sweeping changes in legislation at the federal level, significant changes have been taking place in the health care sector.

The chapters in this volume address some important aspects of health care reforms, including Medicare reform, managed care and its effect on the health care system, efforts to cover the uninsured, the effect of health insurance on labor market and employment decisions, and the role of tax policy in health care in the past and the future. While conducting sound and solid economic analyses of health care issues, the authors of the chapters all recognize the political implications as well. This political economy approach puts the discussion of health care reforms in the proper perspective, since health care involves many stakeholders and its reforms inevitably have political as well as economic repercussions.

Medicare reform is central to health care reform efforts, because more than 39 million people currently get insurance and health care through Medicare. As Medicare is tax financed, its reform is extremely difficult economically, and politically as well. Len Nichols's chapter explains these difficulties and contrasts two leading proposals for

Medicare reform, one from the current congressional health policy leadership and the other from the Clinton administration.

Nichols identifies two fundamental sources of Medicare's long-run financial strain. One is purely demographic; there were 3.9 workers per beneficiary in 1998, but there will be only 2.3 by 2030. The other source of strain is cost growth; while overall health care costs in the United States have been rising as a share of income, Medicare costs have been growing even faster than general health care costs for the past 30 years. Simplified calculations indicate that some payroll tax increase is inevitable as the share of our population over 65 increases in the first half of the twenty-first century. Nichols proposes that the key to minimizing this tax increase is to control the rate of growth in costs per beneficiary, and that the cost reduction can only be accomplished by a fundamental restructuring of incentives for beneficiaries, health plans, and fee-for-service Medicare. The principles of structural reform are to offer beneficiaries incentives to choose lower-cost health plans and health service delivery arrangements, and to make health plan pricing policy efficient. However, efficient plan-pricing systems that are available to large private companies may not work well in Medicare, because Medicare confronts additional constraints such as concerns for geographic equity and income equity.

Having stated the principles for Medicare reform, Nichols then evaluates two major proposals that emerged in 1999, the Breaux-Frist proposal, which grew out of the Bi-Partisan Commission's plan, and President Clinton's plan, which was a response to the former. The two proposals share some important principles. First, they both have competitive price incentives for beneficiaries, plans, and fee-for-service Medicare. Second, both proposals make prescription drugs an optional part of the Medicare benefit package. Finally, both have provisions that protect low-income and high-risk individuals and address geographic cost differences. However, the two proposals differ in their treatment of three key features: the amount of the government contribution toward health plan enrollment choices by beneficiaries, use of national averages to influence local competition, and adjustment for geographic differences in price and utilization to Medicare beneficiaries. An example constructed by Nichols indicates that, in general, the Breaux-Frist proposal imparts stronger incentives for health plan efficiency. However, beneficiaries would pay more on the margin for all private plans under Breaux-Frist. Finally, Nichols points out that major health care policy changes can only be achieved with a broad bipartisan consensus, and he outlines a compromise that could result from the two proposals.

Another aspect of the health care system that has attracted a lot of attention in recent reform efforts is managed care. Managed care developed out of various efforts to contain costs in the 1970s and 1980s, as health care costs increased rapidly during that period. The growth of managed care has raised important questions about its impact on the well-being of patients and the structure of the medical care system in general. Much of the public debate about these issues has been conducted using opinions and anecdotes. In his chapter titled "Managed Care and Social Welfare: What Has Managed Care Really Done to the U.S. Health Care System?", Laurence Baker provides and synthesizes evidence on the impacts of managed care on care, outcomes, satisfaction, and expenditures of patients, as well as on the overall structure and functioning of the health care system. A large number of studies have produced some consistent and convincing conclusions. In terms of treatment, the studies find that managed care patients use the hospital less than patients in indemnity plans. As managed care imposes restrictions on patient choices and other inconveniences, HMO enrollees are less satisfied with their plans than enrollees in other types of plans, primarily indemnity or preferred-provider organization plans. However, research on health outcome on the whole fails to find a consistent pattern either for or against managed care. Finally, studies on expenditures frequently report that managed care patients spend less on health care than patients in indemnity plans.

Baker then reviews evidence about the impact of managed care on the overall health care market, because the presence of managed care in an area may influence care for patients enrolled in other plans—the so-called "spillover effect." These studies find that overall spending and spending for non–managed care patients is lower in areas where managed care has a high market share. Studies also suggest that managed care can influence the number and types of providers, the capacities of the health care system, and the ways in which the system is organized. For example, researchers report that areas with high HMO market share had fewer hospital beds in the mid and late 1980s, that managed care prompted consolidation in provider markets, and that managed care slowed the adoption of many technologies, particularly high-cost, infrastructure-intensive new technologies. Again, there is little evidence on health outcomes from these market comparison studies. Based on the findings about the impact of managed care on the health care system, Baker raises a number of important questions about the future development of the health care system. How will managed care affect the development of the delivery system; for instance, technology advancement and the training of medical professionals? To what extent can managed care further reduce medical costs? These questions have important policy implications.

Jonathan Gruber addresses health care reforms from a different perspective and asks what should and can be done to provide health insurance to the uninsured in the United States. Despite expansions in the Medicaid program in the past 15 years, there are more than 43 million people uninsured, representing over 18 percent of the non-elderly population. In his chapter, "Covering the Uninsured: Incremental Policy Options for the United States," Gruber first identifies who the uninsured are in the United States. Then, drawing lessons from Medicaid expansion efforts across the United States over the past 15 years, he discusses a number of policy options to extend coverage to the uninsured, and their effectiveness and efficiency.

Of the 43 million uninsured in the United States, almost 11 million are children. Nearly 60 percent of the uninsured are in families where the head of the family is a full-time, full-year worker. This fact has motivated continued efforts to increase coverage through the expansion of employer-provided insurance. Based on cost-efficiency arguments, Gruber proposes that the government should pursue a "filling the cup from the bottom" policy that places priority to those groups that have little other recourse to insurance. The policy should encourage efforts to make insurance available to those who are already eligible for Medicaid but have not taken it up. Further expansions of public insurance up the income scale can certainly extend coverage to the uninsured and is an approach taken by the recent Children's Health Insurance Program (CHIP). One problem with this approach, however, is that the coverage may be extended to people who already have private insurance. To mitigate this crowd-out effect, state programs can take advantage of the flexibilities built into the CHIP by making the benefits less generous than Medicaid and introducing premiums and co-payments for services. Incremental changes in tax subsidies can also extend coverage to some of the uninsured. The current system of tax subsidies leaves three groups without subsidies for the purchase of health insurance: those who work for firms that do not offer health insurance, those who are neither employees nor self-employed, and those who work for firms that do not offer a Section 125 plan that allows employees to contribute their share of health insurance premiums on a pretax basis. Recently there have been a number of proposals to expand the tax deductibility of health insurance. Gruber points out that expansive tax policies may not be able to increase coverage to a sizable fraction of the uninsured. Moreover, generous tax credits may induce those who have group insurance to switch to highly subsidized nongroup insurance. Insurance portability and other mandates and insurance market reforms can also reduce the number of the uninsured. However, Gruber cautions that although private insurers are free to raise premiums, government interventions generally will not be effective in extending coverage to the uninsured.

Health care reforms are complex because changes in the health care system may affect other aspects of the economy in a significant way. For instance, types of health insurance and their availability have important implications to labor market behavior of individuals as well as firms. Brigitte Madrian's chapter explains the link between the health insurance market and the labor market, and how health insurance arrangements affect decisions regarding employment, retirement, and career changes. Madrian first points out that, of the many pieces of the health insurance system in the United States, the most significant one is employer-provided health insurance, which provides coverage to 64 percent of the non-elderly U.S. population. Because some types of health insurance are provided as a condition of employment while other types are more readily available when individuals are not employed (for example, Medicaid), health insurance has an important impact on the decision of employment itself. Madrian estimates that individuals with access to retiree health insurance leave the labor market about 6 to 18 months earlier than those who do not have access to such insurance. These individuals are also more likely to retire before the age of 65. Moreover, individuals with access to retiree health insurance are much more likely to make a gradual transition from work to retirement than those without retiree health insurance. As the fraction of employers offering retiree health insurance has fallen by almost half over the past 15 years, and some Medicare reform proposals consider to raise the Medicare eligibility age from 65 to 67, it is predicted that these changes are likely to increase the average retirement age. Based on her own and other research, Madrian asserts that health insurance institutions also affect unskilled single mothers' decisions on working or taking welfare, married women's decisions on participating in the labor force, and decisions on changing jobs and self-employment.

Health insurance may also affect the labor demand decisions of employers. The fixed-cost nature of health insurance gives firms an incentive to reduce the labor costs by hiring fewer employees at longer work hours and fewer but more productive employees. Similarly, as part-time workers are exempt from the nondiscrimination rules as required by the tax treatment of employer expenditures on health insurance, employers may choose to hire part-time workers in lieu of full-time workers as a way to economize on insurance costs. Madrian concludes that because there have been significant changes in the health insurance market in the United States over the past 15 years, it is important to understand the relationship between health insurance institutions and the labor market, and to evaluate the impacts of health care reforms on the labor market and the economy as a whole.

Catherine McLaughlin's chapter in a way is a complementary piece to Madrian's, as it provides more detailed evidence regarding how firms and consumers make their choices under the current health insurance system in the United States. Ninety percent of the firms with 100 or more employees choose to offer some kind of health insurance to their workers, while less than half of the firms with less than 10 employees choose to do so. Small firms are less likely to offer employees health insurance mainly because of the high premium relative to their revenues; they typically face higher premiums than larger firms. Another reason for not offering health insurance is that employers believe that workers can get health insurance from their spouses and may wish to trade health insurance for higher wages. Indeed, a survey conducted by McLaughlin and Zellers reveals that in firms where employers responded that their employees' ability to get insurance elsewhere was an important reason for not offering insurance, 73 percent of the employees did obtain health insurance from other sources.

McLaughlin also finds that higher paid workers are much more likely to be offered health insurance. Only 43 percent of workers earning less than $7 per hour are offered health insurance by their employers, whereas 93 percent of those earning more than $15 per hour are offered. The availability of another source of insurance enables workers to choose employment in small businesses that do not offer employee health insurance, or simply choose not to participate in the employer-provided insurance. Of the workers who choose not to participate, 75 percent have other group coverage, usually through a spouse's plan. Finally, of those workers who participate in the employer-provided health insurance, half of them have no choice in plan; most are offered only a traditional fee-for-service plan. About one-third of those who have choice in plans are offered one or more managed care plans. For many workers, the choice of their employers determines the choice of plans.

As health care is either directly financed by taxes, such as Medicare and Medicaid, or subsidized by certain tax exemptions, such as employer-provided insurance and insurance for the self-employed, health care reforms inevitably involve tax policy. Robert Helms's chapter discusses the role of tax policy in shaping the health insurance and health care markets and its implications to health policy reforms. Helms asserts that tax policy since World War II contributed significantly to both the rate of growth of private health insurance and many attributes of its structure and performance. In particular, tax policy caused group health insurance to grow at a much faster rate than individual insurance. He argues that the tax treatment of health insurance introduces inefficiencies into the health markets, increases the costs of health insurance and medical care, and makes it more difficult for low-income workers and the self-employed to purchase health insurance. In view of recent policy debates, Helms notes that the serious proposals to reform the health insurance market have one feature in common; they all involve some variation of tax credits. He then evaluates the effectiveness of the proposed tax credit programs by referencing several studies by health economists. He primarily focuses on the elasticity studies to evaluate how health insurance expenses respond to tax credits. He concludes from these studies that a tax credit will be more effective in reducing the number of the uninsured than a tax deduction. A refundable tax credit will be more effective in reaching relatively more of the low-income than a flat dollar tax credit. In addition, it seems that low levels of tax credit will have relatively small effects on the purchase of health insurance.

The chapters in this volume reflect the opinions of six leading health economists on certain important issues of health care reforms in the United States. While they can only cover part of the complex health care reforms, they all conduct insightful analyses of the issues concerned, in terms of economic consequences and political implications that changes in the health care system will bring about. The analytic frameworks and the insights provided in this volume will be valuable for understanding and evaluating further developments of health care reforms, which will surely remain a central issue of the U.S. public policies for years to come.

1

The Not-So-Simple Economics (and Politics) of Medicare Reform

Len M. Nichols
The Urban Institute

Despite an unprecedented amount of policy attention since 1995, the U.S. Congress has been unable to agree upon an approach to long-term or structural Medicare reform. This chapter will explain why Medicare reform is important but difficult, both economically and politically. It will contrast the two leading proposals for Medicare reform, from the current congressional health policy leadership and the Clinton-Gore Administration, respectively. This chapter concludes with a brief discussion of a possible compromise that could be crafted from these proposals, if the political will and leadership is forthcoming after the 2000 elections.

THE IMPORTANCE OF MEDICARE

Medicare is our most sacred social contract precisely because it binds the generations together with the promise to pay for the health care needs of the elderly today in exchange for the expectation that future generations will pay for the needs of the current generation of workers. In 1965, when the Medicare program began, only about half of the elderly had any health insurance. Insurers were reluctant to sell to the elderly who manifested health problems, and the poverty rate was sufficiently high that many elderly simply could not afford insurance even if it was priced with actuarial fairness. Public intervention was absolutely essential for all seniors to have access to insurance and care. Today, over 39 million people get insurance and health care

9

through Medicare, and of these, 34 million are aged and 5 million are nonaged disabled.

Medicare is also an extremely important income support program for health care providers. Figure 1 shows the percent of revenue from different types of providers that is derived from Medicare. Hospitals and home health agencies are obviously dependent upon Medicare, and physicians and nursing homes are seriously affected by Medicare payment policies as well. Thus, providers are major stakeholders as well as beneficiaries and taxpayers. This fundamental duality of the Medicare program—an insurance program for the elderly and severely disabled as well as an income support program for all major providers—makes the politics of Medicare reform even more complicated than it would otherwise be.

THE LONG-RUN FINANCING CRISIS

Since Medicare is mostly payroll-tax or income-tax financed, there are two fundamental sources of Medicare's long-run financial strain.

Figure 1 Medicare's Share of Provider Revenues

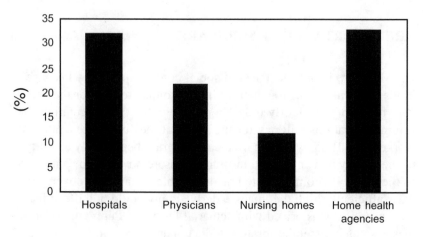

SOURCE: Health Care Financing Administration Office of the Actuary, 1998 data.

The first is purely demographic: there were 3.9 workers per beneficiary in 1998, and by 2030 there will be only 2.3. The second source of strain for Medicare is cost growth. Medicare costs, in the aggregate and per beneficiary, have grown even faster than health care spending in the United States generally. These two facts require that unless some structural change is implemented, the Medicare program may become unsustainable in the future.

Figure 2 puts the cost growth problem into some perspective. It shows total national health expenditures (NHE) as a share of gross domestic product (GDP), Medicare's share of NHE, and Medicare's claim on GDP. As most readers know, health care is a normal good: as incomes rise, most people and societies purchase more of it; thus, it is not surprising that NHE/GDP has grown from about 7 percent in 1970 to over 13 percent in 1998 as the promise and efficacy of medical treatment has absorbed increasing shares of our national income growth. The relative growth of Medicare spending is illustrated through the increasing share of NHE and of GDP that it claims, almost doubling and more than tripling, respectively, from 1970 to 1998.

Comparing Medicare to general NHE on a per enrollee or per capita basis is perhaps most instructive. Medicare costs per beneficiary

Figure 2 Shares of Health and Revenue Related to GDP

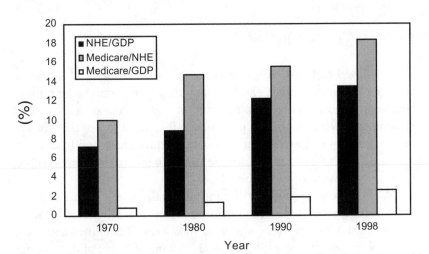

SOURCE: Health Care Financing Administration, Office of the Actuary.

have grown in real terms—over and above general inflation—at slightly more than 5 percent per annum since 1970. Overall NHE per capita, by contrast, has grown at 4 percent per year. Thus, while overall health care costs have been rising as a share of income and in real terms, Medicare costs have risen even faster than general health care costs for the last 30 years.

A bit of slightly oversimplified algebra will make clear the stark nature of the long-term Medicare financing problem.[1] Let B = the number of elderly beneficiaries, c = the expected costs of covered health service per beneficiary, p = the fraction of those costs paid for by beneficiaries through premium payments, w = the average earnings of workers, L = the number of workers in the society, and t = the payroll tax rate required to finance the Medicare program. In equilibrium, program costs in a pay-as-you-go insurance program like Medicare are completely financed by beneficiaries and taxes

Eq. 1 $cB = pcB + twL.$

Now the total population (T) is divided into the share that is young and ineligible for Medicare (y), and the nonyoung ($1 - y$) who are. Only some fraction of the young (f) work. Therefore $L = fyT$, and $B = (1 - y)T$. Substitution into Equation 1 and solving for t, the required payroll tax rate, yields

Eq. 2 $t = [(1 - p)c/w][(1 - y)/fy].$

The first bracketed term represents the publicly financed Medicare costs per dollar of average earnings, and the second term is the ratio of beneficiaries to workers. The required tax rate increases with both of these ratios. Note that health policy can affect only two of the five key parameters in our pay-as-you-go tax rate equation: p, the fraction of Medicare costs that beneficiaries are asked to pay in premiums, and c, the average covered cost per beneficiary.

As our society ages, y will continue to decline. So unless labor force participation increases enough to offset this, fy will continue on its current downward path (as it is for most OECD countries and some developing countries as well). Then at least one or more of three things must happen: 1) growth in cost per beneficiary must be curtailed, 2) the fraction of covered health costs borne by the elderly and their families must increase; or 3) the payroll tax rate must increase. Clearly, the more success we have with the first, the less political pain we must inflict with the second and/or third.

To illustrate the order of magnitude of the problem we face, if we hold p constant at today's level (9.8 percent) and current growth trends continue for all variables on the right-hand side of Equation 2, the required payroll tax rate t will increase from today's implicit 5.5 percent to 14.4 percent in the next 20 years.[2] A doubling of the current beneficiary share, p, reduces the required tax rate in 2018 to only 13.2 percent. Given the nature of our political discourse over the last few years, it is hard to imagine that double-digit payroll tax rates for Medicare alone will ever be politically acceptable, at least not in the first one-third of the twenty-first century.

Reducing annual real growth in cost per beneficiary from the historical 5 percent to 3 percent <u>and</u> doubling the beneficiary premium share would bring the required payroll tax rate down to 8.9 percent by 2018. As a final example, if we were somehow able to reduce the annual real growth in costs per beneficiary to 1 percent, then we could keep p on its current trajectory to 12 percent and the payroll tax rate would have to rise to a level no higher than 6.6 percent.

One important inference from this set of exercises is that some payroll tax increase is inevitable and reasonable to expect as the share of our population over 65 increases in the first half of the twenty-first century. Another lesson is that controlling the rate of growth in costs per beneficiary is the key to minimizing that tax increase, which will surely remain a goal even as we preserve our commitment to all the elderly. This chapter focuses on alternative paths to reduce the growth in c, the Medicare-covered health services cost per beneficiary.

PRINCIPLES OF STRUCTURAL REFORM

We have established that the fundamental goal of long-term Medicare reform is to reduce the real rate of growth of costs per beneficiary. This can only be accomplished by a fundamental restructuring of incentives for beneficiaries, health plans, and fee-for-service (FFS) Medicare as well.

Beneficiaries must have incentives to choose lower-cost health plan and health service delivery arrangements, or plans and providers will have no incentive to become more efficient. The simplest way to impart these incentives is to take serious steps toward implementing market principles—letting low-cost providers charge beneficiaries less, and requiring high-cost providers to charge beneficiaries more—while assuring that quality remains within acceptable bounds. There may indeed be a natural trade-off between cost and quality, but the basic idea behind structural Medicare reform is to allow beneficiary preferences to play a larger role in defining the appropriate place along that trade-off than they have in the past, rather than relying exclusively on executive branch determinations and dictates pursuant to legislative instructions.

In addition, policymakers have to define other trade-offs with efficiency, like those with equity arising from income differences—price incentives contradict ensuring access for the poor, for example—or risk differences. Ultimately, legislation determines how much people of different income and health risk will pay on average, though the Health Care Financing Administration (HCFA) could be given the assignment to create incentives within certain bounds as defined by Congress and the White House together. Finally, the complex issue of appropriate geographic adjustment could present a set of subtle and not-so-subtle trade-offs. Pursuing payment and benefit equity across the country may be impossible in a geographically heterogeneous nation like ours, where not only payment rates but utilization patterns vary tremendously as well. We will return to geographic adjustment issues again in the proposal section, for they are among the thorniest in Medicare reform.

Incentives for private plans to become efficient providers of acceptable or higher quality care would also be easier to implement through a new pricing system than any other known way. In many ways, structural Medicare reform is really about how to get health plan pricing policy right. Today it is highly inefficient because payment is formulaic and administered and is based ultimately on FFS Medicare costs. This is not a linkage that promotes efficient behavior by either health plans or FFS providers, and thus is not in the long-run interests of either Medicare beneficiaries or taxpayers.

A short digression is worthwhile at this point to clarify that managed care is consistent with the original intent of the architects of Medicare. A fair reading of the legislative history of the Medicare program indicates that the original intent was to provide our elderly with the same kind of health insurance that most workers were offered. In 1965, that was indemnity coverage for FFS medicine, typically through a Blue Cross-Blue Shield plan. Today, the private industry norm is some kind of managed care. Thus, Medicare actually lags the private sector by quite a bit in moving most of its beneficiaries to managed care.

In my view, some form of managed care is here to stay, notwithstanding the increasingly emotional debate about patient protection acts in the current Congress that reflects the current backlash over cost-control techniques. Now, some managed care policies and plans surely need changing, but to argue that we can do away with care managers trying to balance cost and quality in clinically appropriate ways is to delude ourselves that 1) all health providers and styles of care are equally outstanding, and 2) we have unlimited resources to spend on health care in this country. Both propositions are patently false, and stakeholders that oppose managed care—for example, physicians who want their unquestioned autonomy and higher incomes back, hospitals who want to charge what they want in order to avoid changing the way they are organized, and politicians willing to exploit a small number of genuine horror stories for political gain—are exaggerating the problems of managed care to further their own self-interests.

That said, ensuring that quality can be properly valued in the Medicare marketplace will not be easy. Advances in measurement are occurring, but there is still much work to do by plans, providers, and beneficiary/family education specialists alike. This work is vital to the future of a competition-driven health system. But while we may wait for the perfect set of quality measures to be devised, to do nothing and just trust unmanaged FFS medicine to solve all our quality and resource allocation problems is clearly not the answer either, as the recent Institute of Medicine report shows (Kohn, Corrigan, and Donaldson 2000).

Trying to make health plan pricing policy more efficient also creates two other types of trade-offs: conflicts with special missions of providers and perhaps of the Medicare program itself, and geographic equity. Academic medical centers that train our future health professionals and conduct the clinical research that improves medical practice—such as teaching hospitals, hospitals that have historically provided a disproportionate share of uncompensated care to the poor and the uninsured, and hospitals that are the only source of medical care in some semirural areas of the United States—all provide more or less public goods for which competitive market forces will always underpay. But forcing health plans to become more efficient through Medicare payment reform will reduce their ability to implicitly subsidize these activities. The wise thing to do would be to take the funding for these activities out of Medicare and Medicaid and have a clear and honest debate about how much research, teaching, uncompensated care, and rural provider support we want to provide, and then fund these activities directly with public funds, federal, state, and local. But wisdom and U.S. health policy are not often included in the same sentence, and while the Balanced Budget Act of 1997 took an important step by removing some graduate medical education payments from Medicare payments to health plans and instead paying them directly to teaching hospitals, providers of these public goods have strong incentives to resist fully efficient Medicare pricing policy until some alternative funding stream for most of their current special activities can be assured.

Geographic equity is also complicated by a zealous pursuit of efficiency. Basically, efficiency would require that prices be set locally at the minimum level to attract services from efficient providers of acceptable quality. But given the geographic heterogeneity of the U.S. health care system and the statutory principle that beneficiaries should pay a premium equal to a fixed percentage of the costs of average Medicare (ambulatory, or Part B) benefits, local efficiency would make it impossible to charge beneficiaries the same amount nationwide. But absolute geographic equity—defined as spending the same amount of money per beneficiary nationwide—would also be problematic, because the same money would buy very different amounts of health care in different parts of the country. Thus, balancing geography and efficiency requires judgment about a complex trade-off, and this issue is one in which the major Medicare reform proposals differ substantially, as we shall see in this chapter.

ALMOST IDEAL MEDICARE
HEALTH PLAN PRICING SYSTEM

Given the principles of structural reform, a useful conceptual experiment might be to ignore the real world constraints on the Medicare program for a moment and discuss the larger features of an almost ideal pricing system, and then examine how the constraints on Medicare do and do not force deviations from the ideal.

In many ways, the best example of an organized health plan purchaser for Medicare to emulate is that of a large, multistate employer with nationwide union contracts that force benefit packages to be equivalent everywhere. Health care, like politics, is local, and private employers do not seem to be troubled by this; they just adapt their health plan arrangements to fit local conditions within the context of their company-wide labor–management agreements. The simplest way to start, and a way that Medicare could surely emulate, is to define a standard benefit package that will be purchased everywhere. In the modern world of twenty-first century health care, that package should include reasonable prescription drug coverage in addition to the current statutory Medicare benefit package. Health plans would then be asked to bid on this package. The government payment amount would be fixed near the middle or lower end of the bid distribution, and beneficiaries would have to pay extra out of their pockets to enroll in high bidding plans. This competitive bidding arrangement would encourage all plans to become more efficient so that they could bid lower and offer premium rebates to attract beneficiaries. Again emulating the best private purchasers today, Medicare would collect and disseminate comparative quality data on plans and their affiliated providers, for this would give beneficiaries the maximum feasible information on which to base their enrollment decisions. Finally, after some reasonable time for remedial action, Medicare would exclude plans and providers who failed to meet acceptable quality or performance targets.

This sort of almost ideal health plan pricing system would have three main virtues. First, it would impart maximum incentives for health plans to become more efficient over time. Second, it would guarantee access to the same set of benefits nationwide. This is in contrast to today, where beneficiaries in Miami get zero premium (above their statutory Part B payment) prescription drug coverage through Medicare Plus Choice plans, and beneficiaries in Minneapolis have to pay large amounts out of pocket to get plans to offer prescription drugs to them, all because the current payment formulas are based on local FFS costs and practice patterns and make very little analytic sense. The third advantage of an almost ideal health plan pricing system is that it allows Medicare to price all health plans locally and avoid the thorny problems of deriving and administering geographic adjusters, which are inherently imperfect.

There are two major risks of the almost ideal health plan pricing system. First, while it does guarantee standard benefits nationwide, it cannot guarantee that beneficiaries will pay the same premium everywhere for the same benefit package. In fact, only one plan in each region is likely to have only the statutory premium attached. Higher bidding plans will have to charge a premium, and lower bidding plans can offer beneficiaries rebates off their statutory amount. This should encourage health plans to become more efficient, but it is not what some analysts and advocates mean when they talk about Medicare being available to all at one nationwide premium for all beneficiaries. Now there are regional disparities today for both availability and price of extra benefits beyond the current parsimonious (excluding drugs) Medicare benefit package, and at least one plan in each area will be available at the statutory price. But if regional disparities in premium payments for most Medicare health plans become too large, then a reevaluation of the definition of the Medicare "entitlement" may be demanded and appropriate.

The second major risk of an almost ideal Medicare health plan pricing system is that it does depend completely on local competition to engender efficient bids. If that local competition is not forthcoming (in rural areas, for example) or not sustainable (if health plan consolidation leaves oligopoly or monopoly health plans in certain areas), then some other way to generate pressures for efficiency must be found.

CONSTRAINTS ON MEDICARE

Even if the almost ideal health plan pricing system could be implemented and made to work well everywhere, Medicare is not and cannot ever be exactly like a large multistate employer. A private employer can strive for efficiency with no worries about spillover consequences, such as provider availability for 39 million beneficiaries, many of whom are very vulnerable and some of whom are chronically ill or disabled, both of which are fairly rare occurrences among working families that employers usually cover.

First, precisely because of these chronically ill and disabled, as well as rural beneficiaries, Medicare cannot ignore FFS providers the way large employers can now if they so choose. Only about 15 percent of beneficiaries are in Medicare + Choice plans today, thus managed care capacity will have to be expanded quite a bit before FFS can be allowed to fade away. Given the preponderance of FFS enrollees today, Medicare simply has to modernize this part of the program as well, rather than just focus on health plan payment policy and wait to achieve efficiency gains until all beneficiaries choose the new and improved managed care plans. Modernization will require selective contracting, performance requirements, and locally negotiated payment discounts with doctors and hospitals, none of which are features of the Medicare program today, and all of which are features of organized private purchasers who do a credible job of managing more or less FFS delivery systems (e.g., preferred-provider organizations).

Medicare must also worry about this problematic geographic equity because it is a national program. There is no simple scientific test to decide if having the same benefits everywhere or charging the same premium everywhere is the better definition of geographic equity. The very idea of geographic equity may be a bit problematic in a country with the heterogeneous health care systems that the United States has. Given that some form of geographic adjustment in payment rates is necessary, it is also difficult to come up with factors that are truly exogenous to local health care system demand. For example, nurses' wages are clearly input prices to both hospitals and doctors' offices, so a geographic adjustment factor including their wages makes intuitive sense. But nursing wages are higher where the demand for health care is greater, so they are hardly a purely exogenous reflection of the relative costs of providing medical care in different places around the country.

The Medicare program must also worry about income equity more intensely than private employer purchasers of health insurance. Low-income Medicare enrollees cannot be expected to bear high out-of-pocket costs, either for health plans or for health services. Since approximately 30 percent of Medicare beneficiaries have incomes below poverty (Moon, Waidmann, and Storeygard 2000), payment provisions for protections that may impede the pursuit of efficiency must be made.

Similarly, differential health risks, while present in relative terms in all insurable populations, may be more of a problem in Medicare than in other settings. For health plans, the absolute financial consequences of being saddled with a disproportionate share of the highest risks are more severe, and thus provisions for risk adjustment of premium dollars received by plans are essential. Equally essential is absolute guaranteed open enrollment and the absence of risk-related beneficiary premiums and co-pays so that no one with chronic or serious illness is prevented from getting medically necessary care.

ALTERNATIVE REFORM PROPOSALS

Since 1995 there have been quite a few proposals to restructure Medicare,[3] and in 1999 two major proposals emerged to galvanize the debate and to act as magnets or centers of gravity for rather different perspectives around which to coalesce. I label these the Breaux-Frist and Clinton proposals, respectively, after the leading politicians who have sponsored them. Breaux-Frist grew out of the Bi-Partisan Commission's plan, which was released in March.[4] President Clinton's plan was developed as a response to the Bi-Partisan Commission plan and was released in July.[5] Specific legislation has now been drafted and some details have been changed, though no formal bill has been marked up in committee and actually voted on in either chamber. Still, the key contours I will outline have not changed, and they will serve to clarify these alternative approaches to long-term structural reform of the Medicare program.

First, I will highlight the important principles that the proposals share. To begin with, they both have competitive price incentives for beneficiaries, plans, and FFS Medicare. This is one essential key for long-run Medicare reform to promote efficiency and thus to reduce the long-run real rate of growth of cost per beneficiary. Second, both proposals make prescription drugs an optional part of the Medicare benefit package. The acknowledgment that prescription drugs are central to modern medical practice is important, even though neither drug provision is as generous as those made outside the context of structural Medicare reform in the bidding wars for the 2000 presidential election campaign. Finally, each major proposal has provisions that would protect low-income and high-risk individuals, as well as address the thorny issue of geographic cost differences. These are important areas of agreement, and they suggest that a compromise is possible within this broad outline.

But the Breaux-Frist and Clinton proposals differ in their treatment of three key features: the reference price, or the amount of the government contribution toward health plan enrollment choices by beneficiaries; use of national averages to influence local competition; and adjustment for geographic differences in price and utilization or patterns of delivery of health care services to Medicare beneficiaries.

The Reference Price

Each reference price is best understood in the context of each proposal's specific and unique bidding process. For Breaux-Frist, there are two benefit packages: core and high-option. Core includes only current law benefits, and high-option adds (at least) an $800 (actuarial value) drug benefit and (at most) a $2,000 stop loss (maximum beneficiary out-of-pocket payment). Health plans must submit a high-option bid, and they may submit a core bid as well if they are willing to sell a package with just current law benefits (all bids in all proposals are presumed to be for the average risk enrollee, and both proposals assume risk adjustments will be made before payments are made to plans). HCFA, as the manager of FFS Medicare, must offer a core bid everywhere in the United States. This bid must be set to break even, i.e., finance itself, over the year. HCFA must also partner with any willing private insurer to offer a high-option plan wherever firms are willing to sell the supplemental policy to go along with its core package of FFS services.

The Medicare board computes the core bid for each plan that did not submit one on its own, and then computes the national weighted average (NWA), an enrollment-weighted average of all bids for the core plan nationwide. For the NWA calculation, each bid is also deflated by its geographic adjuster, as determined by the board. (The geographic adjuster will be explained in some detail later, for this is the third key element wherein Breaux-Frist differs from Clinton).

The Breaux-Frist reference price is 88 percent of the NWA for core plans and $0.88 \times$ NWA + 25 percent of the statutory minimum cost of the drug benefit ($800) for high-option plans, or $0.88 \times$ NWA + 200. If a core plan bid exactly the NWA, the beneficiary would have to pay $0.12 \times$ NWA to enroll in it. If a high-option plan bid exactly the NWA + 1,000, the beneficiary who chooses it would pay $0.12 \times$ NWA + 1000 $- 0.25 \times$ Drugcost $= 0.12 \times$ NWA + 800. (This paragraph assumes the geographic adjuster and the risk adjuster for that beneficiary are each 1.0 for simplicity of exposition).

The larger point is that this type of reference price builds in both carrots and sticks; high-bidding plans must charge more than these reference amounts, and plans that bid less could offer beneficiaries discounts. Thus, this kind of pricing structure imparts strong incentives for plans to become efficient or lose market share.

Clinton also has core and high-option benefit packages, but they are structured somewhat differently than in Breaux-Frist. The core defined benefit is the current law package plus zero cost sharing on a specific set of prevention benefits. The high-option package adds a specific outpatient prescription drug benefit (no deductible, 50 percent co-insurance up to $5,000 in drug spending) to the Clinton core. HCFA would add the prescription drug benefit to the "high-option" FFS plan. Private plans must bid a price at which they are willing to supply each package. Plans could also add the cost of reducing regular Medicare cost sharing, as long as this does not increase the actuarial value and cost by more than 15 percent.

HCFA and/or FFS Medicare do not bid, per se. Yet the reference prices for the Clinton proposal are pegged at 96 percent of the local

FFS cost for the core package and at 96 percent of the FFS cost of the core package plus the cost of HCFA-administered drug benefit. This has the effect of insulating beneficiaries who choose FFS from ever paying more than the statutory part B premium amount, i.e., beneficiaries under Clinton's plan will always be able to select FFS without a financial penalty for FFS's inherent inefficiency at controlling costs. However, low-bidding plans will be able to offer premium rebates to beneficiaries, with beneficiaries getting 75 percent of the savings and the government getting 25 percent of the savings. In this way, the Clinton reference price structure is all carrots: since FFS is expected to usually be the highest-cost plan, private health plans have incentives to bid low to gain market share but no stick forcing them to bid low to be competitive as the NWA provides under Breaux-Frist.

Use of National Averages to Affect Local Competition

Breaux-Frist uses the NWA as a check on local plans and on FFS Medicare. Breaux-Frist also uses the local bids to force FFS Medicare to become more efficient or lose market share. (This will become a bit more clear in the examples I present below). Clinton uses the FFS premium guarantee to protect beneficiaries while still offering plans the reward of higher market share for competing successfully (at lower cost) against FFS Medicare. Clinton's proposal also has plans to modernize FFS, i.e., make it more like a preferred-provider organization.

Adjustment for Geographic Differences

The third major difference between the proposals for long-term Medicare reform is treatment of geographic cost differences. Breaux-Frist would adjust bids only for local input price differences. This approach is consistent with a particular view of utilization differences: that they are clinically unjustified and mostly driven by ignorance of best medical practice or pursuit of economic gain by providers. Clinton's original proposal called for "full" geographic adjustment, which seemed to promise to adjust for all FFS utilization differences as well as price differences among different areas. But the final proposal as specified in the FY2001 budget documents defined the geographic adjuster as an enrollment-weighted average of FFS and managed care costs, locally as compared to national averages, which at least allows for managed care utilization to dampen slightly the degree for which utilization differences are adjusted. The Clinton approach is consistent with a view that most, if not all, utilization differences among areas are legitimate—more or less the opposite of the Breaux-Frist view.

The significance of these divergent views is made clear in Table 1, which decomposes Medicare + Choice payment rate deviations from the national average into input price and utilization sources in eight different metropolitan statistical areas. I used the simple hospital wage index to proxy input prices. The table shows that areas that cost more than the national average, from Trenton to Miami, could mostly have high utilization (the Florida locations), high prices (Los Angeles and Flint), or just slightly elevated utilization (Trenton). Areas with below average costs (Tacoma and South Bend) have substantially lower utilization, even sufficiently low enough to more than counter the effect of higher prices (Tacoma). The point of this table is to suggest, however, that the Breaux-Frist geographic adjuster will have very different effects and be much more popular in Los Angeles and Tacoma than in Miami. Clinton's adjuster, on the other hand, is likely to be the most popular of the two adjusters everywhere, which is no doubt why it was designed precisely the way it was.

Table 1 Geographic Disparity in Medicare Managed Care Plan Costs

	2000 Medicare + Choice payment ($)	% above U.S. avg.[a]	% due to price HWI[b] – 1	% due to utilization
Miami	724.23	43.4	2.3	40.2
Ft. Lauderdale	623.63	23.5	1.7	21.4
Palm Beach	564.73	11.8	–0.5	12.4
Los Angeles	627.76	24.3	20.9	2.9
Flint	576.49	14.2	10.2	3.6
Trenton	521.93	3.4	–0.4	3.8
Tacoma	439.62	–12.9	16.3	–25.1
South Bend	415.86	–17.6	–2.1	–15.9

SOURCE: Author's analysis of Health Care Finance Administration data. Price deflator is the hospital wage index.

[a] The U.S. average is $504.96.

[b] Hospital wage index.

EXAMPLES TO HIGHLIGHT THE DIFFERENCES
IN THE BREAUX-FRIST AND CLINTON PLANS

The following hypothetical examples are designed to illustrate how the competing proposals would translate a given set of "facts," i.e., private health plan bids and FFS costs, into marginal prices that beneficiaries would pay, and thus, ultimately, into incentives for long run efficiency. It is not simple to construct an example that permits an "apples to apples" comparison across reform proposals because they have different benefits in their "high-option" plans and because their treatments of FFS Medicare are so dissimilar—Clinton does not force HCFA to bid per se, whereas Breaux-Frist requires it to break even with its premium collections. Nevertheless, the following is offered as a first order approximation of an example that permits a fair comparison, and while I have made some simplifications compared to the "actual" proposal throughout (these proposals are moving targets in any event), I have been careful to preserve the rank order of beneficiary premiums that would actually occur among plans and geographic areas.

I use four "plans": two private HMOs (Plans 1 and 2), FFS Medicare, and FFS Medicare with a high-option supplement (FFS + D), where D = prescription drugs. Both private plans offer each proposal's high-option package: the implicit assumption to keep the premium bids identical under both Breaux-Frist and Clinton is that the more expansive drug benefit under Clinton has the same actuarial value as the drug benefit plus stop loss in the Breaux-Frist high-option package. Table 2 lists the bids by each plan in a low-cost and a high-cost area. (A high-

Table 2 Bids of Sample Plans ($)

	Low-cost area	High-cost area
Plan 1	6,100	8,300
Plan 2	6,710	8,930
FFS	6,200	6,200
FFS+D	7,300	7,400
NWA	6,000	6,000

cost area is presumed to have 10 percent higher prices and 20 percent higher utilization than the national average. A low-cost area is presumed to have 5 percent lower prices and utilization). NWA is the national weighted average computed under the Breaux-Frist rules.[6]

Table 3 shows the reference prices in the low-cost and the high-cost areas (for the Clinton plan, the reference prices are relevant to plans 1 and 2 since this reference price includes drugs for the high-option plan). Note that the Clinton reference prices are uniformly higher in the same geographic area. This shows the protection Clinton gives to FFS, while Breaux-Frist provides stronger incentives for health plans to become more efficient.

Table 4 shows what beneficiaries would pay out of pocket on the margin for each of the specific health plan choices in the example. Recall that, under the Clinton plan, beneficiaries pay the Part B premium for FFS without drugs. I proxied this amount by making it equal to 10 percent of the nationwide FFS average cost in my example, or $620 per year. Note that the Clinton plan would charge beneficiaries less for all plans in the low-cost area, and considerably less for private plans in the high-cost area, because the Clinton reference price is so high. However, and perhaps surprisingly, Breaux-Frist would charge beneficiaries less for standard FFS than Clinton.

Table 3 Reference Prices, Given Example Bids ($)

	Low-cost area	High-cost area
Breaux-Frist	5,700	6,600
Clinton	6,642	8,943

Table 4 Beneficiary Payments, per Year, per Beneficiary ($)

	Low-cost area		High-cost area	
	Breaux-Frist	Clinton	Breaux-Frist	Clinton
Plan 1	920	863	2,220	638
Plan 2	1,530	1,388	2,850	1,107
FFS	1,220	620	320	620
FFS+D	2,120	1,120	1,320	1,120

This result illustrates the power of the NWA versus the Clinton reference price. In high-cost areas, FFS is relatively cheap under Breaux-Frist since it is forced to bid the national average everywhere, and by definition the national average FFS is lower than the average cost in high-cost areas. The NWA formula makes FFS even more attractive. The Clinton proposal, on the other hand, keeps the absolute price of FFS the same everywhere, and the surprising result is that because of the way the Clinton reference price is computed (with geographic adjusters, not shown but available from the author on request), the private health plans are actually cheaper in high-cost areas—to beneficiaries—than they are in low-cost areas. This is in some ways an artifact of this particular example, wherein excess utilization is more important in defining the high-cost areas than excess prices, but as Table 1 showed, this is also a fair representation of Florida's high-cost Medicare markets in real life.

The upshot of this example is that because Clinton adjusts area-specific reference prices for utilization differences and input prices, whereas Breaux-Frist only adjusts for input prices, Breaux-Frist imparts in high-cost areas much stronger incentives on high-cost private health plans to become more efficient, or they will be hard pressed to survive in high-cost areas. Now high-cost areas—which are, after all, high-cost because of their historical FFS utilization and pricing patterns—are where the greatest potential for new savings lie, as efficiencies are sought. Thus, Breaux-Frist imparts the strongest incentives for private plans to become efficient in the areas where it is likely to do the most good from a program-wide efficiency perspective. Clinton, by contrast, ends up protecting the excess utilization in high-cost areas by making private plans here relatively inexpensive compared to FFS + D, until this protection is eroded by the slightly declining geographic adjuster over time as costs elsewhere (note the low cost area's private premium bids) reduce the geographic adjustment factor over time. It is clear from Table 4 that health plans in high-cost areas would greatly prefer the Clinton approach. In absolute terms, they would prefer Clinton in low-cost areas as well, though relative to FFS, private plans under Breaux-Frist are better off than under Clinton.

IMPLICATIONS OF THE EXAMPLE

In general, Breaux-Frist imparts stronger incentives for health plan efficiency. Private plans in high-cost areas—especially if utilization is the main reason they are high-cost now—would have to become much more efficient very quickly or charge such high premiums they would likely lose business to FFS. Indeed, the NWA calculation works in such a way that FFS Medicare seems relatively cheap in high-cost areas. Beneficiaries would pay more on the margin for all private plans under Breaux-Frist, and for HCFA's FFS plan with prescription drug coverage. In the example, the NWA also works to make the out-of-pocket cost of FFS exceed the price of the lowest-cost plan in low-cost areas, which implies that managed care plans might be encouraged to enter here, since they could likely compete against the national average-priced FFS plan.

As advertised, the Clinton plan protects FFS beneficiaries well, in that FFS Medicare, offered to them for the usual Part B premium, is the lowest-cost plan in each type of area. In the example, no private plan bid lower than the Clinton FFS plan, but private plans were cheaper than Clinton's FFS plan that includes prescription drugs. Thus, beneficiaries who wanted prescription drugs and were price conscious in both high-cost and low-cost areas would be able to find non-HCFA alternatives to their liking. In a surprising reflection of the implications of "almost full" geographic adjustment, the out-of-pocket premium for the private plans with drugs is lower in the high-cost areas under Clinton than in the low-cost areas. From the point of view of encouraging beneficiaries to migrate to managed care in high-cost areas, this is good. But the Clinton approach, relative to Breaux-Frist, is clearly going to discourage managed care growth in low-cost areas. It also may stall significant growth in high-cost areas as well, since it will be hard to provide the extra benefits beneficiaries want (e.g., outpatient prescription drugs) and also to price below FFS Medicare, especially if FFS Medicare modernizes along the lines of the Clinton proposal. Of course, if managed care cannot control cost growth better in the long run, then it should not—and would not—grow relative to FFS. The Clinton plan does a better job overall of hedging the bet that managed care is destined to win this competition.

Each plan has both potential and obvious flaws. In my judgment, the Clinton plan's incentives are potentially weak in high-cost areas. Especially to the degree that norms of excess utilization are responsible for historically higher than average costs in these areas (as in Miami, etc.), there may be much more inefficiency to wring out of the system than the Part B premium allows room. Recall, the Clinton plan is all carrots. Thus, plans can price lower than FFS but they can't go below zero, and FFS doesn't have to charge more when it's more expensive than the reference price, as in Breaux-Frist. Thus, a potential private plan premium discount relative to FFS costs—the Part B premium, or roughly 10 percent of national average FFS costs in the example—is constrained to be no more than $620 in 2000.

The Breaux-Frist plan, by contrast, may have too harsh an incentive structure. It would clearly be disruptive in the short run in high-cost areas, precisely where managed care enrollment within Medicare is highest today. Ironically, if imposed without a transition phase as the plan was originally drafted, it would likely kill off Medicare managed care plans in precisely the areas where Medicare needs managed care to help it save resources in the long run. The complement to this effect is that the NWA protects FFS in these high-cost areas, which is unlikely to be wise for long run Medicare payment policy.

OUTLINE OF A COMPROMISE

These implications, relative strengths, and flaws of each Medicare reform proposal all point to a fairly obvious compromise that might actually make decent long-run policy sense: start with the Clinton plan and gradually wean FFS from this much protection by lowering the reference price over time to something closer to the Breaux-Frist concept. The wisdom of reforming Medicare deliberately as opposed to precipitously should be obvious.

In the long run, a locally defined contribution based on competitive bidding makes perfect sense, as does making FFS Medicare compete. But FFS Medicare must be given time to modernize, and payment reform should not kill off any options in year one, or there will be precious little competition and reform in the long run. It seems likely that

Medicare will need both sticks and carrots in its ultimate pricing arsenal—as Breaux-Frist has—to achieve the lowest possible c (real growth in per beneficiary costs). It would be wise to reevaluate the Clinton concept of more or less full utilization adjustment, though recent work by Cutler and Sheiner (1999) suggests that zero utilization adjustment is probably not appropriate either, and truth may be closer to two-thirds than some people now think. Finally, to make all Medicare health plan pricing reforms palatable, Medicare must work hard on quality measures and plan accountability. Ultimately, the limit to how aggressive pricing reforms can be will be set by how much the people in the United States trust the health care delivery systems we allow Medicare to pay for.

LIMITS OF ECONOMIC ANALYSIS
OF MEDICARE REFORM

To conclude, it is important to remember that Medicare is not just an abstract set of incentives that may be oddly structured for economists' tastes. Economists can best serve the Medicare debate by identifying the trade-offs inherent in competing policy objectives and real world conditions, and in analyzing the likely outcomes of alternative incentive structures. That is, at best, economics merely clarifies the choices real policymakers face. If we have learned anything in Washington during the eight years of the Clinton Administration, it is that major health policy changes, as structural Medicare reform would be, can only be achieved with a broad bipartisan consensus. Only with this consensus can entrenched interests—which will always oppose reform—be overcome. However, the other lesson that economic analysis can offer Medicare reformers is that the cost of delay is higher future pain (in tax rates) and hasty, ill-considered implementation snafus and unintended consequences. That is surely a poor enough bargain to keep minds in Washington concentrated on Medicare reform.

Notes

I am very grateful to David Cutler, Mark Miller, Bob Donnelly, Greg White, Carolyn Davis, Phil Ellis, Mark McClellan, Marilyn Moon, John Holahan, Steve Zuckerman, Josh Weiner, Stu Gluterman, Anne Mutti, Mike O'Grady, Kathy Means, Nora Super Jones, Jeff Lemieux, Stuart Butler, and Bob Reischauer for many helpful discussions about the issues raised in this chapter and concerning Medicare reform generally. All errors remain my sole responsibility. All opinions in this chapter are my own and do not represent those of the Urban Institute, its trustees, or its sponsors.

1. This algebra section is taken from Nichols (2000). I simplify a bit by assuming there are no non-elderly disabled beneficiaries, no elderly workers, and that all public funds are financed with a payroll tax. Including the precise details would complicate the algebra without changing the essential point at all, since the general fund financing that reduces the actual required payroll tax rate also increases the fraction of income tax revenue that must be dedicated to Medicare. Nevertheless, the stylized "t" that is calculated in this simplified example is higher than is actually required because of current income tax financing and because of the payroll and income generated by elderly workers.
2. Author's calculations; details available on request.
3. Reischauer, Butler, and Lave (1998); Moon (2000); Helms (2000). See also the papers by McClellan, Cutler, Fuchs, Reinhardt, and Saving in the Spring 2000 issue of the *Journal of Economic Perspectives*.
4. The bipartisan commission's proposal can be found at http://medicare.commission.gov/medicare/index.html. Breaux-Frist was introduced in the U.S. Senate as S. 1895 in November of 1999.
5. The Clinton plan can be found in the FY2001 budget documents. Contact the author for further details.
6. Under Clinton, the FFS plans do not bid, per se, but under Breaux-Frist they do.

References

Cutler, David M. 2000. "Walking the Tightrope on Medicare Reform." *Journal of Economic Perspectives* 14(2): 21–44.

Cutler, David M., and Louise Sheiner. 1999. "The Geography of Medicare." *American Economic Review* 89(2): 228–233.

Fuchs, Victor R. 2000. "Medicare Reform: The Larger Picture." *Journal of Economic Perspectives* 14(2): 57–70.

Helms, Robert B., ed. 2000. *Medicare in the Twenty-first Century: Seeking Fair and Efficient Reform*. Washington, D.C.: AEI Press.

Kohn, L.T., J.M. Corrigan, and M.S. Donaldson, eds. 2000. *To Err is Human: Building a Safer Health System.* Washington, D.C.: National Academy Press.

McClellan, Mark. 2000. "Medicare Reform: Fundamental Problems, Incremental Steps." *Journal of Economic Perspectives* 14(2): 21–44.

Moon, Marilyn, ed. 2000. *Competition with Constraints: Challenges Facing Medicare Reform.* Washington, D.C.: Urban Institute Press.

Moon, M., T. Waidmann, and M. Storeygard. 2000. "Differences in Estimates of Poverty for Medicare Beneficiaries: Comparing the MCBS and the CPS." Photocopy, Urban Institute, Washington, D.C.

Nichols, Len M. 2000. "Managing the Medicare Insurance Market." In *Medicare in the Twenty-First Century: Seeking Fair and Efficient Reform,* Robert B. Helms, ed. Washington, D.C.: American Enterprise Institute Press.

Reinhardt, Uwe E. 2000. "Health Care for the Aging Baby Boom: Lessons from Abroad." *Journal of Economic Perspectives* 14(2): 58–71.

Reischauer, Robert D., Stuart Butler, and Judith R. Lave, eds. 1998. *Medicare: Preparing for the Challenges of the 21st Century.* Washington, D.C.: National Academy of Social Insurance.

Saving, Thomas R. 2000. "Making the Transition to Prepaid Medicare." *Journal of Economic Perspectives* 14(2): 85–98.

2

Managed Care and Social Welfare

What Has Managed Care Really Done
to the U.S. Health Care System?

Laurence Baker
Stanford University
and
National Bureau of Economic Research

For most of the last century, the U.S. health care system was financed primarily through traditional indemnity health insurance plans that paid doctors, hospitals, and other health care providers on a fee-for-service basis. By the 1960s, most Americans received insurance of this type through either their employers or government programs, such as Medicare and Medicaid (HIAA 1991). In the midst of economic prosperity that minimized constraints on the revenues they could collect, and faced with the then comparatively low cost of health care, health insurers and the government provided ample funding for the widespread provision of ever more advanced health care. In the process, this subsidized and encouraged the training of new physicians, the building of new infrastructure, and the development of increasingly advanced, and almost always more expensive, technologies. By all accounts, these developments contributed significantly to the capabilities of medicine to cure disease and improve the health and functioning of patients. By the 1970s and 1980s, though, rapidly increasing costs gave rise to a number of cost-containment efforts. Perhaps the most prominent of these efforts is the growth of managed care, encompassing a range of changes in the practices of health insurers that have eroded the pillars of the traditional fee-for-service health care financing system.

The growth of managed care has raised important questions about its impact on the well-being of patients. An increasing number of opponents argue that expansion of managed care has put cost cutting front and center, displacing concerns about quality and health, and will inevitably harm patients and reduce the well-being of the U.S. population. But this view may not be completely correct. Advocates of managed care argue that fee-for-service medicine fostered waste and inefficiency, and that by developing better methods of allocating resources, society can obtain the same value from its health care system for less money. Moreover, maintaining the traditional health care financing system was increasingly costly, and savings generated by managed care can also contribute value to society.

Much of the public debate about the impact of managed care has been conducted around opinion and anecdote, without careful analysis of the large body of evidence available on the impact of managed care on health care, outcomes, and costs. This chapter aims to contribute to these debates by presenting and synthesizing key evidence, seeking to evaluate what is known about the impact of managed care on the well-being of the U.S. population. The first sections briefly discuss the origins and definition of managed care and present a framework for analyzing the impact of managed care on the well-being of society. The next section reviews evidence on treatment patterns, outcomes, satisfaction, and expenditures in managed care organizations. Following that is a discussion of the impact of managed care on non–managed care patients and on the structure and functioning of the health care system in general. The next section presents some supplementary evidence on cost savings from growth in managed care. The final sections synthesize the evidence presented, discuss welfare implications, and consider the future of managed care.

WHAT IS MANAGED CARE AND WHERE DID IT COME FROM?

The health care system that grew up in the United States after World War II was a lavishly funded affair. With a strong economy, it was relatively easy for employers to include generous indemnity health insurance in employee compensation packages. These insurance plans typically provided broad coverage of health care spending with no restrictions on the physicians or hospitals used by the beneficiaries, provided for little oversight, if any, of the treatment decisions made by physicians, and placed few restraints on the amounts that could be charged. Free spending in the private sector was augmented by extensive public sector spending in the form of the Medicare and Medicaid programs, providing fee-for-service coverage for the elderly and poor, as well as programs like the Hill-Burton program for the development of hospital infrastructure, and the National Institutes of Health for medical research.

Although financial incentives are not the only force that influences the health care delivery system, they can play an important role in shaping the system's institutions and behavior. It is perhaps not surprising that the health care system that grew up in this environment reflected, in at least some ways, the financial forces that nurtured it. With few financial constraints, it was easy for providers to supply their patients with many advanced services. Under many traditional indemnity plans, neither the patient nor the provider bore any of the cost of treatment, so one would expect providers and patients to demand all services that would have had even some probability of a benefit for the patient, even those that were very costly to the insurer and to society. Moreover, the inclination to do everything possible for patients was reinforced by the fact that providers paid on a fee-for-service basis received additional compensation for furnishing more—and more expensive—services. Because increasing numbers of patients had insurance, these incentives helped to ensure the availability of advanced medicine to broad segments of the population.

Beyond influencing the treatments provided for individual patients in a physician's office or hospital, the availability of generous compensation for providing extensive and expensive care with the latest techniques also influenced the infrastructure of medicine. It attracted new medical students who ultimately contributed to the increasing number of physicians, particularly specialists; it fostered the development of new hospitals; and it encouraged the adoption of new techniques and equipment, in turn creating a ready market for the purchase of new innovations that helped fuel a large and active research establishment.

All of this contributed to the formation of a health care delivery system that enjoyed wide public support as a world leader, particularly with respect to its advancement and ability to make high-tech care available to broad segments of the population. But, maintaining this system turned out to be a costly endeavor. The United States spent then, and continues to spend now, markedly more than any other country in the world. In 1997, the United States spent 13.9 percent of its gross domestic product on health care, while the next highest figure was from Germany, at 10.7 percent. Other industrialized countries like France (9.6 percent), Canada (9.2 percent) and the United Kingdom (6.8 percent) were even lower (OECD 1999).

As the costs of sustaining the system increased over time, cracks began to appear in the foundation of public support that backed the system. Spending large amounts of money to obtain highly valued items is easily justifiable, but, first in the 1960s and more evidently in the 1970s and 1980s, some began to question whether the value received from the health care system was commensurate with the level of spending. Some of the unease was generated by the fear that additional health care spending was not generating significant improvements in health. Despite leading the world in health care spending, life expectancy, infant mortality, and other population-level indicators of health remained worse in the United States than in other developed countries. Moreover, some evidence suggested that excessive health care, potentially detrimental to health, was being provided. One study found that at least one-third of carotid endarterectomies, surgery to improve blood flow to the brain, were unnecessary and inappropriate, as were at least 17 percent of angiograms, invasive X rays of the coronary arteries (Brook 1989). Both of these procedures carried nontrivial risks to patients, and the knowledge that these and other potentially risky procedures were being overprovided gave further reason for reexamination of the incentives in the system. If it is health that ultimately produces the value society derives from the health care system (a debatable proposition to which I return below), then spending that does not produce health is inefficient and should be redirected to purchase other goods or services that generate value for society.

All of this led to a variety of efforts to mitigate the incentives generated by the traditional insurance system that appeared to be encouraging high spending on things of questionable value. These efforts included things like the widespread introduction of co-payments and deductibles, the imposition of second opinion requirements for elective procedures, and Medicare's Prospective Payment System. Most prominent among them, though, is the growth of managed care, which began in earnest in the early 1970s and reached full swing during the 1980s and 1990s.

The term *managed care* refers collectively to a set of activities that health plans and others can undertake to mitigate the propensity for the provision of more and more expensive services fostered by unmonitored fee-for-service medicine. There are three main managed care strategies. The first is centralization of control over utilization decisions. Fee-for-service medicine was characterized by virtually complete autonomy on the part of physicians and other providers, in consultation with the patient, with respect to care choices. Under managed care, health plans can take on more significant roles in overseeing care choices. For example, patients and their physicians may be forced to obtain preapproval from a utilization review organization for diagnostic tests or surgical procedures if the plan is to pay for the services. Plans can then deny approval for services that they deem to be inappropriate uses of resources. Many plans regulate the use of specialists by forcing patients to sign up with a particular primary care physician or group of physicians and then obtain a referral from this "gatekeeper" physician or group when specialized services are required. Plans can also engage in activities like promulgating guidelines for care or developing detailed formularies of approved pharmaceutical products for which they will pay, effectively limiting prescribing to the approved list. Less direct forms of control are also possible. For example, many plans periodically review the practice patterns of physicians to identify those whose use of services appears excessive, and they may provide incentives for meeting the targets.

Second, health plans can impose indirect controls on utilization by using financial arrangements that put providers at risk for the financial implications of the patient care decisions they make. For example, plans can use capitation contracts in which physician groups (or even individual physicians) are paid a fixed amount per patient per month to care for the patients who have signed up with them. This effectively reverses the fee-for-service incentive to provide more care to each patient. In other cases, plans may withhold a portion of the payments due to physicians and reallocate these funds at the end of the year based on the performance of physicians or groups in meeting utilization, quality, or other targets imposed by the plans.

Finally, health plans may define networks of physicians and health care providers with whom they will work and provide incentives for patients to see only those providers chosen. Defining a panel offers plans the advantage of selecting only those providers with whom they are interested in working, as well as the potential to obtain contracting advantages and discounts from physicians who would like to be included in the panel. Some plans define relatively broad networks of affiliated physicians and providers, while other plans focus their efforts on building relatively narrow panels and carefully managing them to include only those providers whose patterns of practice are most consistent with their goals. Plans that have formed networks can impose restrictions on the ability of patients to choose providers outside of the network. Some plans will not pay for care delivered by physicians or hospitals not included in the approved panel. Other plans provide some financial incentives for patients to see providers in the panel, but they will pay at least part of the bill for out-of-network care.

Beyond the three main categories of plan activities, there is a wide range of other things that plans can do to influence practice patterns. Many plans engage in efforts to change physician opinions about the best ways to care for their patients. They may, for example, provide information and work with physicians to define standards for care. Plans may also influence practice patterns simply by collecting data on the performance of services that the plan or other observers like the National Center for Quality Assurance believe to be indicators of quality.

Today, most health plans use more than one of these techniques, and plans vary widely in the combinations of approaches they use and in the weight they put on each approach. To some extent, different combinations of approaches define the stereotypical organizational forms that are commonly observed in the marketplace. Staff and group model HMOs, like Kaiser Permanente and the Group Health Cooperative of Puget Sound, tend to tightly define a network of providers whose financial incentives are closely aligned with the incentives of the plan and restrict patients to choose only providers in the network. Because the panels are carefully defined and financial incentives are already integrated, there is relatively little need to impose strong central controls on utilization or use financial incentives to limit costs.

Independent practice association (IPA) model HMOs typically have more loosely defined networks of physicians and restrict patients to remain within the network. The looseness of the network and the lack of integration with the plan requires stronger efforts to contain utilization. IPA-model HMOs vary in the emphasis they place on financial incentives as opposed to direct controls, but the prototypical IPA-model HMO relies heavily on some combination of them.

Preferred-provider organizations (PPOs) are characterized by relatively loose panels, some incentives to choose providers in the network (but weaker incentives than those used by HMOs), and limited efforts to control utilization. As a result, PPOs have been regarded as potentially less effective at controlling costs than other organizations. Many formerly unmanaged indemnity plans have also adopted managed care techniques over the past years, typically consisting of efforts to impose some (frequently limited) central control on utilization patterns.

Taken as a whole, the growth of managed care represents a massive shift in the financial incentives at work in the U.S. health care system. Between 1981 and 1998, HMO enrollment grew from 10 million to 105.3 million, with about 30 percent of this growth coming after 1995 (Hoechst Marion Roussel 1999; Interstudy 1994). PPO growth was also substantial, and by some accounts the vast majority of the U.S. non-elderly population was enrolled in some form of managed care plan by the late 1990s.

A FRAMEWORK FOR EVALUATING
THE IMPACT OF MANAGED CARE

Growth in managed care has prompted questions about its impact on the health care system and on the well-being of patients, which could be evaluated from a number of different perspectives. Here, I take society's perspective and attempt to discuss the issues important in determining whether society's total utility, or value, has been increased or decreased by managed care.

Individuals can be characterized as getting utility from three things. First, people get utility from health. Second, people can get utility from the amenities or other attributes of the health care system that do not necessarily improve health but reduce their hassles or increase their enjoyment. People value short waiting times in doctors offices and friendly staff, even if these things do not directly make them healthier. The American public has also expressed a desire for high-tech, advanced care even though this has not always been shown to produce better health than lower-tech, less aggressive medicine. Some people may simply value the knowledge that they are receiving the most up-to-date treatments from the most highly trained specialists. For others, receipt of high tech therapies may foster the perception that health is being maximally improved, even in cases where this is not actually the case. Finally, individuals get utility from the amount of money they have left after their spending on health care, including health insurance, out-of-pocket spending, and spending for any other health care goods and services. I can thus write a representative individual's utility function as

Eq. 1 $u = u(h, a, y - y_h)$,

where h denotes health, a denotes amenities, y denotes income, and y_h denotes spending on health care. Obtaining the maximum amount of utility requires trading off the purchase of more and better health care, which could generate more health and better amenities, with consumption of other things.

Society consists of many individuals, so from society's perspective one can write

Eq. 2 $U = U(H, A, Y - Y_h)$.

For simplicity, society's total utility could be thought of as a summation of the utility of each individual, although in reality it is probably more complicated than that. Thinking about overall social utility, though, produces the same problem for society as for an individual. In order to obtain the maximum amount of collective utility, we must trade off the purchase of more health care with nicer amenities against the use of our collective income for other pursuits.

The social perspective can differ in important ways from the individual perspective. Most notably, focusing on social utility maximization allows for trade-offs between members of society. Foregoing expensive services with low probability of success for some patients, and using the savings to purchase immunizations for others might improve total social utility, but it would be redistributive, producing individual winners and losers. The incidence of costs can also vary among individuals—some may save more or pay more than others toward the collective social spending on health care. Although individual-level analyses of welfare can be interesting and important, the question of overall social benefit or loss is an important question from a general policy perspective, and it is the one I focus on here.

The question, then, is whether social utility is higher or lower in a world dominated by managed care than it would have been in a (hypothetical) world without managed care. In a given time period t, a system dominated by managed care will produce some level of health, amenities, and spending that will yield a level of utility U_t^M. A fee-for-service system would also produce some level of health, amenities, and spending, generating U_t^F. Society is better off with managed care at that point in time if $U_t^M > U_t^F$ and worse off if $U_t^M < U_t^F$.

Since the health care system is continuing to evolve, an evaluation would also do well to take into account both present and future levels of utility, with appropriate discounting to account for the difference between value now and value later. When utilities over time are taken into account, activities that have value now but hurt future value, like cost cutting that produces no current change in treatments but does affect research and hence the prospects for future treatments, would have to be weighed against each other.

Without knowing the specific functional forms, it is impossible to precisely evaluate society's utility or the impact managed care has on it. However, given information about the impact of managed care on health, amenities and patient satisfaction, and costs, we can draw inferences about the likely effects. That is, an informed perspective on this question can be obtained by evaluating any reduction in health and amenities managed care has brought about relative to any savings it has generated. The next three sections discuss the large and growing literature that provides insight into these questions.

TREATMENT PATTERNS, SATISFACTION, AND
OUTCOMES FOR PATIENTS IN MANAGED CARE

One important body of literature compares treatment patterns, health outcomes, satisfaction, and spending for patients who enroll in managed care organizations and those who do not. This literature contains hundreds of studies, and I do not attempt to review them all here. Rather, I summarize the results of several good reviews that synthesize information from the many original studies. Luft (1981) summarized studies done between 1959 and 1975. Miller and Luft (1994) compiled results from studies done between 1980 and 1993. Miller and Luft (1997) compiled results from studies done between 1994 and 1997. Dudley et al. (1998) reviewed work primarily on outcomes done between 1980 and 1997.[1] A wide range of studies are also reviewed in Glied (2000) and Chernew et al. (1998).[2]

The comparison studies discussed here share some general characteristics. First, they almost all focus on patients enrolled in HMOs. This is useful because HMOs are a classic form of managed care organization and are still probably the most aggressive form of managed care organization in the marketplace. Yet, existing studies provide little information about the experience of patients in PPOs or other types of managed care plans.

Second, almost all of these studies attempt to compare patients in HMOs to patients in traditional indemnity plans. This is a sensible comparison group, but it does raise issues because of the general evolution of health plans over the past decade. It is relatively rare now to find even indemnity health insurers that have not adopted some managed care strategies. Earlier studies may thus provide more easily interpretable comparisons than later studies, because the characteristics of the control group in earlier studies are clearer. More recently, studies of Medicare patients may be most useful since Medicare maintains a relatively unmonitored fee-for-service system for its traditional enrollees.

Third, few of these studies are randomized. Most of them examine groups of patients for whom the plan in which they are enrolled is the product of a choice made by the enrollee or by some other entity, like an employer. If the health status, preferences, or other characteristics of HMO enrollees differ from those of other patients, results from comparative studies could be biased. Indeed, a large body of literature suggests that health status does frequently differ between patients in and out of HMOs (e.g., Hellinger 1987, 1995; Glied 2000). Many comparison studies do attempt to control for differences in the characteristics of patients, but the methods used and the quality of the available control variables vary from study to study. One notable exception is the RAND Health Insurance Experiment, a randomized trial conducted in the late 1970s and early 1980s. As part of the trial, 1,149 patients were randomized to join the Group Health Cooperative of Puget Sound, a staff-model HMO, providing a study design capable of avoiding problems with selection bias (Manning et al. 1984).

Despite these inconveniences, this literature does provide an important window into the impacts of managed care, producing a number of very consistent and strong findings. I review evidence on treatment patterns first, followed by satisfaction, health outcomes, and spending.

Comparing Treatments for Managed Care and Non–Managed Care Patients

Managed care patients use the hospital less than patients in indemnity plans. The earliest studies indicated lower hospital utilization stemming from reductions in admission rates (Luft 1981). Work done between 1980 and 1993 frequently finds reductions in length of stay as well. Miller and Luft (1994) reported that HMO hospital admission rates were lower in 8 of 11 studies that presented evidence on admissions, with the most credible evidence suggesting reductions of 26 percent to 37 percent. They also found shorter lengths of stay in 15 of 16 observations in their study, with the strongest evidence suggesting a length of stay reduction of 14 percent. Evidence from the RAND Health Insurance Experiment confirms these results, reporting 40 percent lower inpatient admission rates and total inpatient days among patients randomized to the HMO arm of the trial (Manning et al. 1984). The most recent (nonrandomized) evidence, however, produces a less clear pattern and smaller differences, although there are relatively few recent results on hospital utilization (Miller and Luft 1997).

A common goal of managed care plans is to replace relatively expensive hospital utilization with less expensive outpatient care. Thus, one might expect to see reductions in hospital use offset by increases in outpatient visits. Although early evidence tended to support this view (Luft 1981), more recent evidence is not as clear. Miller and Luft (1994) found higher outpatient utilization among HMO patients in half of the 14 observations they reviewed, and lower outpatient utilization in the others (although the studies they reviewed with the strongest data tended to suggest higher or similar outpatient utilization in HMOs). Miller and Luft (1997) reported no overall pattern in the results of studies done between 1994 and 1997. Evidence from the RAND Health Insurance Experiment also suggested no differences in the overall rate of face-to-face visits (Manning et al. 1984).

A wide range of studies suggest that patients enrolled in HMOs are less likely to get intensive, costly tests and procedures. Miller and Luft's two reviews (1994, 1997) included a total of 24 observations on a range of advanced and frequently expensive services, including treatments associated with childbirth, heart disease, and cancer. They found less use among HMO patients in 22 of the 24 cases. In most of these cases the reductions were relatively large: the modal odds ratio associated with HMO enrollment was about 0.80, indicating that the odds of receiving the intensive procedure were about 20 percent lower in HMOs relative to indemnity plans. Some more recent studies confirm these findings. For example, Chernew, Fendrick, and Hirth (1997) reported lower use of cholecystectomy in HMO patients than indemnity patients at a given point in time.

Interestingly, while many studies report lower use of costly tests and procedures among HMO patients at a given point in time, some research suggests that trends over time are similar in and outside of HMOs (Chernew et al. 1998). For example, Langa and Sussman (1993) found similar growth between 1983 and 1988 in the use of coronary revascularization among HMO and non-HMO patients, although HMO patients use the technology less at any given point in time. Chernew, Fendrick, and Hirth (1997) showed that the change in cholecystectomy use by HMO patients over 1989–1994 was similar to the change seen in the overall health care system.

Studies also suggest that HMO enrollees are also less likely to get access to home health care than indemnity patients. Both Miller and

Luft (1997) and Dudley et al. (1998) identified multiple studies indicating significantly less home health use among HMO patients.

On the other hand, HMO patients are more likely to receive preventive care. Miller and Luft (1994) reported that HMO enrollees consistently receive more preventive tests, including cancer screening, hypertension screening, and a variety of regular examinations. HMO enrollees also receive more health promotion activities, like smoking cessation counseling, than indemnity plan enrollees. Dudley et al. (1998) confirmed this finding with more recent data. Evidence from the RAND Health Insurance Experiment also supports this view, finding higher rates of preventive visits among those randomized to the HMO (Manning et al. 1984).

Comparing Satisfaction for Managed Care and Non–Managed Care Patients

Along with changes in treatment patterns have come many changes in the amenities of the health care system. In pursuit of lower costs, managed care plans have imposed restrictions on patient choice of providers; minimized staff, which has led to shorter visit times and less opportunity for interaction; and placed more burdens on patients to navigate increasingly complex systems for obtaining approval for care. Many patients, along with their doctors, have sought care that was denied, sometimes for reasons that are difficult to understand. Many physicians are dissatisfied with the payment rates of managed care plans. Increasing reliance on gatekeeper physicians and financial incentives that reward physicians for doing less have undermined patient trust in physicians, which can color the perceptions of both patients and physicians. As they have become more prominent, these kinds of changes have led to widespread anecdotal reports of dissatisfaction and backlash among patients and providers.

Consistent with these reports, studies that assess overall patient satisfaction almost always find that HMO enrollees are less satisfied with their plans than enrollees in other types of plans, primarily indemnity or PPO plans (Miller and Luft 1994, 1997; Dudley et al. 1998). This overall finding is not surprising, but it has two important nuances that should be noted. First, studies that separately identify satisfaction with financial and nonfinancial aspects of health plans typically find the greatest discontent in nonfinancial areas. HMO enrollees systematically report being less satisfied with things like the technical proficiency of the care they received, their relationships with clinicians, the amount of time spent with clinicians, and access and availability of specialists. On the other hand, HMO enrollees are frequently more satisfied with the financial aspects of their plans. Managed care plans frequently require less out-of-pocket spending than indemnity plans with potentially high deductibles. Managed care plans can also require less paperwork to handle for insurance reimbursement than indemnity plans.

Second, studies that focus on lower-income populations, many of which have joined HMOs under emerging Medicaid managed care programs, frequently find that HMO enrollees are more satisfied with both financial and nonfinancial aspects of their plans. This may be understandable given that many of these patients are covered by Medicaid, and fee-for-service Medicaid has historically been very difficult to navigate. Outside of Medicaid, lower-income groups seeking low premiums can end up in high-deductible or other stringent plans that do not offer much care to enrollees.

Comparing Health Outcomes for Managed Care and Non–Managed Care Patients

On the whole, the literature on health outcomes fails to find a consistent pattern either for or against HMOs. Studies from the 1980s and early 1990s tend to suggest equal or better quality of care in HMOs. Fourteen of 17 observations summarized by Miller and Luft (1994) showed HMOs to be the same as or better than indemnity plans on a range of measures, including care for patients with congestive heart failure, colorectal cancer, diabetes, hypertension, cerebrovascular accident, or chronic problems like joint pain and chest pain. Only a few observations suggested worse quality of care in HMOs.

But, this pattern disappears in more recent work. Miller and Luft (1997) reviewed a number of articles that examined outcomes ranging from mortality to measures of physical functioning among patients with specific serious health conditions, to more general measures of patient health applicable to the broad population. Some of the studies reviewed found better outcomes in HMOs, including studies showing

HMO enrollees having lower risk of ruptured appendix, lower risk of dying in the intensive care unit, lower breast cancer mortality, better stage at diagnosis of cancer, better physical functioning (as measured by activities of daily living [ADL] and instrumental activities of daily living [IADL] scales), better glycosylated hemoglobin levels among diabetics, and better mental health functioning. On the other hand, a number of studies found worse outcomes in HMOs, including studies reporting higher mortality rates among breast cancer patients and high-risk newborns, as well as worse physical and mental health functioning among chronically ill patients and elderly patients. In between, a large number of studies reported no pattern of different results or a mixture of findings favorable and unfavorable to HMOs.

Of 35 observations considered by Dudley et al. (1998) comparing mortality, clinically significant morbidity, and laboratory abnormalities, most found no significant differences between HMOs and indemnity plans. Among the few that did find significant differences, there was no clear pattern favoring either HMOs or indemnity plans. Dudley et al. (1998) also reviewed several studies of process of care measures. Here, although a number of studies found differences between HMOs and indemnity plans in one direction or another, there was also no clear pattern favoring one over the other.

This literature supports the general view that there is not a systematic effect of HMOs on outcomes. In particular, there is no clear evidence that population outcomes are systematically worse in HMOs. That said, though, it is important to note that there are some subgroups of the population that evidence suggests may be affected. First, although the literature is not unanimous, there is some evidence that outcomes are worse among vulnerable populations in HMOs (e.g., Ware et al. 1996), which may give rise to concern for their well-being. Second, there are some particular conditions for which outcomes in HMOs appear to be worse and others for which outcomes appear to be better. Drawing the general conclusion that there is no systematic effect of HMOs based on population-wide evidence from a number of different conditions implicitly assumes that each of society's constituent subgroups and all health conditions should carry equal weight in an overall assessment. But this need not be the case. Society may find it desirable to put more weight on the health outcomes of some members of the population, like the socioeconomically disadvantaged, or give more weight to those who suffer from some diseases and less to those who suffer from others. In this case, a thorough evaluation would need to aggregate results for each population group and condition, weighting by measures of their significance. Developing a scheme to weight conditions and carrying out such a calculation is beyond the scope of this chapter and will have to be left for future study.

The fact that the literature does not support the view that outcomes are systematically worse in managed care plans may be something of a surprise given the extensive news coverage devoted to the adverse impacts of managed care on health. But, it is important to remember that bad things happened to undeserving patients under fee-for-service too. In some cases, it is likely that this was the result of overprovision of care encouraged by the financing system, although such events were rarely reported in the press and were certainly not linked to the health insurance system in place at the time.

It is interesting to note that the earliest studies suggested better outcomes in HMOs than outside, but this pattern fades with time. One (although not the only) interpretation of this finding is that the spread of managed care has influenced treatment patterns throughout the market, leading differences between HMOs and other plans to disappear over time as the other plans come to more closely resemble HMOs.

Comparing Expenditures for Managed Care and Non–Managed Care Patients

Studies of expenditures by HMO and indemnity patients frequently report that expenditures are lower in HMOs. Miller and Luft (1997) reported that the majority of the studies they reviewed showed lower total spending on health care for HMO patients than fee-for-service patients, with spending differences ranging from 16 percent to 34 percent. Earlier data are sparser, but the two studies reviewed by Miller and Luft (1994) that provided information about total spending reported spending by HMO enrollees to be 11–13 percent lower than spending by fee-for-service patients. Note that these expenditures include spending by the plan on health care received, not the premiums paid for coverage or other costs. From society's perspective, expenditures for care are perhaps the more important dimension to consider.

While most of the evidence available focuses on HMOs, there is some limited evidence on expenditures for PPO patients, but it ends up mixed. Smith (1997) suggested that PPO patients have lower expenditures than indemnity patients, but Hosek et al. (1990) found that PPOs have higher unit costs.

EVIDENCE FROM MARKET LEVEL STUDIES

Additional information about the impacts of managed care is available from studies that compare the performance of the health care system in market areas with high levels of managed care activity and market areas with lower levels. The approach taken in these kinds of studies is to classify markets[3] based on the overall level of managed care activity, frequently measured as HMO market share (i.e., the proportion of the population enrolled in an HMO), and then examine differences in the structure of the health care delivery system, treatments, costs, and outcomes in markets with varying levels of market share.

One important aspect of market level studies is exploration of the so-called "spillover effects" of managed care, by which the presence of managed care in an area influences care for patients not enrolled in managed care plans. This could occur through a variety of mechanisms. Managed care could influence the structure of the health care delivery system or its capabilities. For example, markets with high levels of managed care activity could end up with more outpatient surgery centers and fewer MRI machines, which could influence the treatment options available even to non–managed care patients. The presence of managed care could also influence the treatment choices of physicians if managed care plans disseminate information or otherwise influence physician practice patterns, and this information reaches physicians who care for non–managed care patients.

Comparing Expenditures among Markets

Expenditures are by far the most common focus of market comparisons (see, e.g., Baker 1997, 1999; Clement et al. 1992; Feldman et al. 1986; Gaskin and Hadley 1997; Noether 1988; McLaughlin 1987,

1988; Robinson, 1991, 1996; Rodgers and Smith, 1995; Welch, 1994).[4] Most of these studies focus on overall expenditures, including expenditures by both managed care and non–managed care patients, but some include only expenditures by non–managed care patients to explicitly explore the potential for spillover effects on spending. Many of these studies focus on in-hospital spending, although some of them examine broader measures that encompass spending on outpatient and other care. Using whatever measure, though, these studies by and large report that overall spending and spending for non–managed care patients is lower in areas with high levels of market share. In particular, more recent studies clearly suggest that the presence of managed care in an area reduces overall hospital expenditures and spending for fee-for-service Medicare beneficiaries.

Interpreting the results of these studies is complicated by the fact that expenditures are the product of price and quantity, so lower expenditures could reflect change in one or the other or both. Some of the evidence is consistent with the view that treatment patterns have changed, so that patients in high managed care areas (even non–managed care patients) receive fewer intensive treatments and fewer hospitalizations. Medicare hospital expenditures, for example, should not be strongly subject to variation in price since the Prospective Payment System centrally determines prices. Hence, the most natural interpretation of studies that show reductions in Medicare inpatient spending associated with higher managed care activity (e.g., Baker 1997, 1999; Clement et al. 1992; Rodgers and Smith 1995) is that practice patterns have shifted so that patients receive fewer hospitalizations and fewer intensive tests and procedures. Some direct evidence supports this finding. Baker et al. (2000b) and Heidenreich et al., (2000) reported that treatments for fee-for-service Medicare patients who suffered acute myocardial infarctions varied with the level of area HMO market share.

Outside of Medicare, it is more plausible that increased managed care activity led to reductions in the prices charged by hospitals and other providers, which could contribute to reductions in overall expenditures in some of these studies. Some studies suggest that increased competition between hospitals can reduce expenditures (Chernew et al. 1998), and that the presence of managed care plans can enhance competition (Kessler and McClellan 2000; Feldman et al. 1990).

Comparing Infrastructure and Capabilities among Markets

A range of market comparison studies suggest that managed care can influence the number and types of providers, the capabilities of the health care system, and the ways in which the system is organized. In most cases, these studies report that the characteristics of high managed care markets reflect the changes in care patterns that managed care brings about. Consistent with findings that managed care plans tend to use hospitals less, Chernew (1995) reported that areas with higher HMO market share had fewer hospital beds in the mid and late 1980s. Consistent with the view that managed care plans are apt to use less care overall and refer their patients to specialist physicians less often, Escarce et al. (1998, 2000) and Polsky et al. (2000) reported that high managed care areas attract and retain fewer physicians, particularly specialists. Consistent with the fact that managed care plans tend to selectively contract with a limited number of providers to obtain many services for their patients, Baker and Brown (1999) reported that managed care prompted consolidation in the mammography market. Managed care may also contribute to consolidation in other provider markets. Burns et al. (2000) reported that physicians and hospitals in markets with more HMOs (although not higher market share) were more likely to form alliances between 1993 and 1995 compared to those in markets with fewer HMOs.

Evidence also supports the view that managed care has slowed the adoption of many technologies, particularly high-cost, infrastructure-intensive new technologies. Baker and Wheeler (1998) and Baker (forthcoming) suggested that high managed care areas saw slower adoption of MRI equipment over the 1980s and 1990s. Baker and Phibbs (2000) suggested that managed care slowed the adoption of mid-level neonatal intensive care units (NICUs). Cutler and Sheiner (1998) reported that managed care is associated with slower diffusion of a range of hospital-based technologies. Cutler and McClellan (1996) showed that high managed care areas adopted cardiac revascularization services at slower rates between 1984 and 1991. This literature is not unanimous, however. Baker and Spetz (1999) reported no differences in an index of hospital technologies between higher and lower managed care areas, and Hill and Wolfe (1997) reported mixed effects of managed care on diffusion of a range of technologies in Wisconsin during and after a transition to managed care dominance.

Comparing Health Outcomes among Markets

There is relatively little evidence on outcomes from market comparison studies. The evidence that does exist concurs with that discussed earlier, namely, that there is not a body of work clearly showing that managed care has systematically worsened outcomes. Baker and Brown (1999) examined breast cancer stage at diagnosis and mortality rates in high and low managed care areas and found no significant differences. Baker et al. (2000b) examined mortality rates for acute myocardial infarction (heart attack) patients and also found no significant differences. Baker and Phibbs (2000) reported that mortality rates for high-risk newborns were probably improved by managed care–induced reductions in the diffusion of mid-level NICUs.

AGGREGATE SPENDING PATTERNS SINCE THE RISE OF MANAGED CARE

Comparisons among plans and among markets suggest that managed care is able to lower expenditures to at least some extent. Another source of information is the patterns in overall health care spending over the time period in which managed care has come to play an important role in the health care system. After rising at an annual rate of more than 10 percent between 1980 and 1990, annual growth in spending slowed to a rate of 4–5 percent between 1994 and 1997,[5] about the time when managed care had grown to the point where it could plausibly be a force in U.S. health expenditures. The slowdown was most pronounced in hospital spending, where annual growth rates fell to just above 3 percent during this time period, consistent with research suggesting that managed care has particularly targeted hospital use. Other areas of spending that do not seem to have been as strong a focus of managed care plans during this period, like prescription drugs, maintained high growth rates.

More recently, however, rates of increase in spending have picked up. Figures for 1998, the most current available at the time of this writing, suggest annual growth in total health care spending was higher than it had been in previous years, although still below the 10 percent increases seen in the 1980s.

SYNTHESIS: ARE WE BETTER OFF OR NOT?

What can all of this evidence together tell us about the impact managed care has had on society? Existing literature supports the view that managed care has significantly shifted practice patterns, reducing the use of the most advanced and intensive treatments and the use of hospitals. These changes appear capable of spilling over to non–managed care patients, who are also treated differently in places where managed care is prevalent. Further, changes in treatment patterns and other incentives accompanying growth in managed care appear to have influenced the structure and capabilities of the medical care system.

There is, however, little evidence that any of these changes have systematically worsened the health of patients. Evidence does support the view that some patients with some conditions have worse outcomes under managed care than fee-for-service, but evidence also suggests that other patients do better. While managed care has not led to overall worse health, it has led to increasing dissatisfaction. Patients are annoyed by a host of factors, including the burdens placed on them in managed care plans, their perception that health care has become more impersonal, their perception (not necessarily supported by the evidence) that the health care they are receiving is of lower quality, their inability to have complete autonomy in the choice of physicians, and their inability to receive all of the care that they might want, particularly the most advanced and expensive treatments.

At the same time, managed care does seem to have produced some savings in the form of lower expenditures on health care. While there is debate about whether or not these savings will persist over time, evidence so far suggests that managed care patients spend less than indemnity patients, that spending is lower in high managed care areas, and that overall U.S. health expenditures grew at slower rates during at least part of the era of managed care.

If managed care does not bring about changes in the health of the population, an assessment of its impact on the current utility of the population depends on the value of the expenditure reductions it produces compared to the value of reduced amenities and satisfaction. At least to this point, evidence would suggest that the net impact of managed care is that we now purchase less fancy and less satisfying health care at a cost that is at least somewhat lower. Society's utility will be higher under managed care than under the former regime if the value of the savings outweighs the value of the lost amenities, and it will be lower if not.

Judging from the public outcry against managed care, it appears that many Americans are unwilling to accept this trade-off. Public backlash against managed care is increasingly evident, and it has prompted numerous regulatory and legislative attempts to inhibit the ability of managed care organizations to engage in activities that they have used to manage utilization, like capitation, utilization review, and restricting choices of providers.

One might wonder, however, about the extent to which the public reaction reflects the results of careful consideration. Many Americans believe that they receive their health care for "free" from their employers or from the government; they do not take into account the true costs of purchasing their health care when they evaluate the costs and benefits of health care proposals. A backlash is understandable when a public is confronted with a reduction in amenities without offsetting savings that are easily recognized, but it need not imply a reasoned conclusion that managed care has lowered utility. Furthermore, many Americans appear to believe that managed care has led to worse health outcomes, a view for which the currently available empirical evidence is not strong. The rejection of managed care might be less pronounced if debate were informed by actual evidence rather than by anecdote and media reports.

On the other hand, there are many informed consumers in the United States, and there has been public debate about health care market changes and health reform proposals for a number of years, frequently highlighting the trade-offs between higher costs, utilization, and amenities. Yet the backlash continues. In some contexts, the debate over President Clinton's health care proposals in 1993 and 1994 was carried out in the framework of a trade-off between encouraging more restrictive managed care in return for savings that could be put to other purposes, like covering the uninsured, and it was rejected. Perhaps in the managed care backlash, Americans—at least some of them—have shown their desire to pay, perhaps in large amounts, to receive the most advanced and expensive health care in the world, even if it does not make them truly healthier.

It is not clear how many Americans fall into this latter category. It is not difficult to believe that much of the managed care bashing observed today is the result of incomplete information about the true effects of managed care. Going forward, informed public debate about the true costs and benefits of managed care could significantly help the country arrive at a consensus about the most useful set of public policy steps to take with respect to managed care.

It would be inappropriate to end this discussion without a comment on the problem of the uninsured. The United States is now, and has for a long time been, burdened with the fact that our health care financing system leaves many people without coverage at all, subjecting them to worse than average health care access and leaving them with much worse than average health outcomes. The advent of managed care has done little to change this, either for better or for worse, so it is not truly a factor in a debate about the impact of managed care on overall utility. At the same time, one of the early hopes for managed care was reductions in spending and premiums and a true community spirit, which might have enabled more employers and individuals to purchase health insurance and contributed to reductions in the rate of uninsurance. In practice, though, this does not seem to have happened.

ASSESSING THE PROSPECTS FOR THE FUTURE

Beyond the impact managed care has had on the U.S. health care system up to this point, there are important questions that it raises about the future development of the health care system. In some ways, these are potentially more important than questions about the impact of managed care to date. Managed care has put us on a path toward the future that is different from the path we would have been on had we continued with the traditional fee-for-service system, and these two paths could easily diverge substantially over the course of time. This section highlights four important issues that will contribute to determining the destination of the managed care path.

First, what effects will managed care have on the future development of the delivery system? Substantial changes in the number and types of providers and the capacity of the system could compound over time and greatly alter the future characteristics of the health care delivery system. One particularly important possibility is that technology advancement will be inhibited. Areas with high levels of managed care are less likely to adopt new technologies and equipment. Fewer potential purchasers for new products may mean less effort devoted to developing new products for market. Managed care also appears capable of influencing the time spent on research. For example, faculty in medical schools have traditionally been an important source of new innovations, but they face increasing pressure in managed care–dominated environments, which may lead them to devote more time to clinical activities and less to their research efforts. Moy et al. (1997) and Campbell et al. (1997) substantiated this possibility, reporting that increases in managed care activity and competition are associated with reductions in the number and dollar amount of research awards obtained by faculty researchers. One of the historical strengths of the U.S. health care system is the level of innovation and new advances that have brought great benefits to patients. Reductions in innovation could have very important implications for overall well-being, albeit in ways that could be hard to assess since we are unlikely to be able to identify the things not invented because of managed care.

While managed care could well alter the path of future innovation, it is important to note that it is unlikely to kill innovation altogether. Managed care plans are unlikely to discourage all innovations; rather, they can be expected to focus most intently on those that they perceive to be cost-ineffective. Managed care may, in fact, substantially reward new innovations viewed as cost-effective. Managed care plans may be able to reward these kinds of innovations much more quickly and substantially than the traditional fee-for-service system because of the influence they can have over utilization decisions. Moreover, managed care plans have not always been able to cut off the use of new and expensive technologies that patients strongly demand (even when they have tried to do so, patients have frequently been able to turn to either the courts or the press to gain coverage of new treatments), making it far from clear that markets for new innovations will dry up under managed care. A survey conducted by Weisbrod and LaMay (1999), in fact, reported that managers of firms involved in research and development do not view managed care as reducing their inclination to conduct research on advanced and expensive new technologies, particularly those that hold the greatest prospects for substantial improvements in medical capabilities.

Beyond technology development, managed care could also alter the future development of other aspects of the delivery system. For example, existing evidence suggests that managed care plans tend to use the intensive services provided by specialists less than indemnity plans, and cross-market comparisons report that areas with high levels of managed care have fewer specialist physicians. Growth in managed care has also fueled powerful discontent among physicians. This suggests the potential for managed care to reduce the number of candidates for medical school, particularly the number of students interested in pursuing specialized career paths, which could leave the future health care system with a very different mix of providers than we currently have and influence the future of patient care.

A second key question with respect to the future impact of managed care is the extent to which costs will be lower. Evidence up until now suggests that managed care has lowered costs at least somewhat. However, this may only consist of one-time savings obtained by squeezing inefficiencies out of the health care system without fundamentally changing the growth path of expenditures. On the other hand, the savings seen so far could reflect a persistent lowering of the future trajectory of expenditures. The dollar difference between these two scenarios is large. If health expenditures continue growing at 3–5 percent per year instead of 10 percent, the accrued savings over time would be much larger than if we return immediately to 10 percent growth rates after having lower growth for four or five years in the mid 1990s.

It is difficult to assess the direction in which costs are likely to go. On one hand, overall spending rose faster between 1997 and 1998 than it had during the preceding three years, consistent with the suspicion that at least some of the savings obtained in the mid 1990s were the results of one-time savings, and that cost growth is tending toward a return to its former high level. On the other hand, the consensus view among economists is that technology growth is the leading driver of increasing health care costs (Fuchs 1996), accounting for as much as half of the rise in expenditures in recent decades (Newhouse 1992; Chernew et al. 1998). As noted above, evidence suggests that managed care can somewhat slow the adoption of new technologies, although the extent to which this will persist is not clear.

A third issue is the extent to which the preferences of the population will evolve. While the U.S. population now appears to strongly value the amenities to which they have become accustomed, preferences could change over time. Patients in the United States may adapt their expectations to managed care and become less concerned about reductions in amenities once they are not so recent in memory. Growth in managed care and increases in the availability of information about objective quality of care may also lead people to place greater value on actual quality and health outcomes than on amenities, which may now be valued in part because there is little other information available on which to base judgements.

Finally, the impact of managed care in the future depends on the characteristics of managed care in the future. The current public backlash against managed care has led many managed care organizations to voluntarily allow more freedom in choosing a provider and impose less oversight on physician decision making. Numerous legislative and regulatory activities aim to further limit the ability of managed care organizations to engage in the practices they have relied upon in the past to manage care. One plausible outcome of this is a weakening of the most aggressive managed care plans and a corresponding return toward previous cost and care trends, for better or worse, over the long run.

Only time will tell, but one can hope that clear discussions among policymakers and the public can help bring about a well-informed consensus about the importance of health, amenities, and health care spending that can guide efforts to improve our health care system as we go forward.

Notes

1. The Luft (1981), Miller and Luft (1994, 1997), and Dudley et al. (1998) reviews make explicit attempts to include only studies meeting certain quality standards, including passing peer review and having included reasonable attempts to control for confounding differences in patient samples.
2. The sets of studies reviewed in these articles are not completely independent. Although there is no overlap between the two Miller and Luft reviews, both Glied (2000) and Dudley et al. (1998) to a large extent overlap the Miller and Luft (1994, 1997) reviews.
3. Cities, defined by the set of Metropolitan Statistical Areas, are the most common unit of analysis, although others are sometimes used (e.g., states or counties).
4. Some additional studies report evidence on premiums (e.g., Baker and Corts 1996; Feldman, Dowd, and Gifford 1993; Wickizer and Feldstein 1995; Goldberg and Greenberg 1979; Baker et al. 2000a; Hill and Wolfe 1997). Some of this work suggests that managed care premiums are lower, or that overall premiums are lower in areas with more managed care, although it is not unanimous. This tends to corroborate evidence suggesting lower overall expenditures, but since premiums can be influenced by cost shifting and other peculiarities of the insurance market, this evidence is not as valuable as evidence on expenditures when assessing the impacts on the overall well-being of society.
5. Expenditure data are from the Health Care Financing Administration's Web site: www.hcfa.gov.

References

Baker, Laurence C. 1997. "The Effect of HMOs on Fee-For-Service Health Care Expenditures: Evidence from Medicare." *Journal of Health Economics* 16(4): 453–482.

_____. 1999. "Association of Managed Care Market Share and Health Expenditures for Fee-For-Service Medicare Patients." *Journal of the American Medical Association* 281(5): 432–437.

_____. Forthcoming. "Managed Care and Technology Adoption in Health Care: Evidence from Magnetic Resonance Imaging." *Journal of Health Economics*.

Baker, Laurence C., and Martin L. Brown. 1999. "Managed Care, Consolidation among Health Care Providers, and Health Care: Evidence from Mammography." *RAND Journal of Economics* 30(2): 351–374.

Baker, Laurence C., and Kenneth S. Corts. 1996. "HMO Penetration and the Cost of Health Care: Market Discipline or Market Segmentation?" *American Economic Review* 86(2): 389–394.

Baker, Laurence C., and Ciaran S. Phibbs. 2000. "Managed Care, Technology Adoption, and Health Care: The Adoption of Neonatal Intensive Care." Working paper no. 7883, National Bureau of Economic Research, Washington, D.C.

Baker, Laurence C., and Joanne Spetz. 1999. "Managed Care and Medical Technology Growth." In *Frontiers in Health Policy Research, Volume 2*, Alan M. Garber, ed. MIT Press: Cambridge, Massachusetts, pp. 27–52.

Baker, Laurence C., and Susan K. Wheeler. 1998. "Managed Care and Technology Diffusion: The Case of MRI." *Health Affairs* 17(5): 195–207.

Baker, Laurence C., Joel C. Cantor, Stephen Long, and M. Susan Marquis. 2000a. "HMO Market Penetration and Employer Health Plan Costs." *Health Affairs* 19(5): 121–128.

Baker, Laurence C., Paul Heidenreich, Jeffrey Geppert, and Mark B. McClellan. 2000b. "The Effect of Area HMO Market Share on Treatments, Costs, and Outcomes for Fee-For-Service AMI Patients." Working paper, Stanford University, Stanford, California.

Brook, Robert H. 1989. "Practice Guidelines and Practicing Medicine: Are They Compatible?" *Journal of the American Medical Association* 262(21): 3027–3030.

Burns, Lawton R., Gloria J. Bazzoli, Linda Dynan, and Douglas R. Wholey. 2000. "Impact of HMO Market Structure on Physician-Hospital Strategic Alliances." *Health Services Research* 35(1): 101–132.

Campbell, E.G., J.S. Weissman, and D. Blumenthal. 1997. "Relationship between Market Competition and the Activities and Attitudes of Medical School Faculty." *Journal of the American Medical Association* 278(3): 222–226.

Chernew, Michael. 1995. "The Impact of Non-IPA HMOs on the Number of Hospitals and Hospital Capacity." *Inquiry* 32(2): 143–154.

Chernew, Michael, A. Mark Fendrick, and Richard A. Hirth. 1997. "Managed Care and Medical Technology: Implications for Cost Growth." *Health Affairs* 16(2): 196–206.

Chernew, Michael E., Richard A. Hirth, S.S. Sonnad, R. Ermann, and A. Mark Fendrick. 1998. "Managed Care, Medical Technology, and Health Care Cost Growth: A Review of the Evidence." *Medical Care Research and Review* 55(3): 259–288.

Clement, Dolores Gurnick, Phillip M. Gleason, and Randall S. Brown. 1992. "The Effects of Risk Contract HMO Market Penetration on Medicare Fee-For-Service Costs: Final Report." Report for the Mathematica Policy Research: Princeton, New Jersey.

Cutler, David, and Mark McClellan. 1996. "The Determinants of Technological Change in Heart Attack Treatment." Working paper no. 5751, National Bureau of Economic Research, Washington, D.C.

Cutler, David M., and Louise Sheiner. 1998. "Managed Care and the Growth of Medical Expenditures." In *Frontiers in Health Policy Research*, Alan M. Garber, ed. MIT Press: Cambridge, Massachusetts, pp. 77–116.

Dudley, R. Adams, Robert H. Miller, Tamir Y. Korenbrot, and Harold S. Luft. 1998. "The Impact of Financial Incentives on Quality of Health Care." *Milbank Quarterly* 76(4): 649–686.

Escarce, Jose J., Daniel Polsky, Gregory Wozniak, Mark V. Pauly, and Philip R. Kletke. 1998. "HMO Penetration and the Practice Location Choices of New Physicians: A Study of Large Metropolitan Areas in the U.S." *Medical Care* 36(11): 1555–1566.

Escarce, Jose J., Daniel Polsky, Gregory Wozniak, and Phillip R. Kletke. 2000. "HMO Growth and the Geographical Redistribution of Generalist and Specialist Physicians, 1987–97." *Health Services Research* 35(4): 825–848.

Feldman, Roger, Bryan Dowd, and Gregory Gifford. 1993. "The Effect of HMOs on Premiums in Employment-Based Health Plans." *Health Services Research* 27(6): 779–811.

Feldman, Roger, Bryan Dowd, Don McCann, and Allan Johnson. 1986. "The Competitive Impact of Health Maintenance Organizations on Hospital Finances: An Exploratory Study." *Journal of Health Politics, Policy, and Law* 10(4): 675–698.

Feldman, Roger, Hung-Ching Chan, John Kralewski, Bryan Dowd, and Janet Shapiro. 1990. "Effects of HMOs on the Creation of Competitive Markets for Hospital Services." *Journal of Health Economics* 9: 207–222.

Fuchs, Victor. 1996. "Economics, Values, and Health Care Reform." *American Economic Review* 86(1): 1–24.

Gaskin, Darrel J., and Jack Hadley. 1997. "The Impact of HMO Penetration on the Rate of Hospital Cost Inflation, 1985–1993." *Inquiry* 34(3): 205–216.

Glied, Sherry. 2000. "Managed Care." In *Handbook of Health Economics*, J.P. Newhouse and A.J. Culyer, eds. North Holland: Amsterdam, pp. 707–752.

Goldberg, Lawrence G., and Warren Greenberg. 1979. "The Competitive Response of Blue Cross and Blue Shield to the Growth of Health Maintenance Organizations in Northern California and Hawaii." *Medical Care* 17(10): 1019–1028.

Health Insurance Association of America. 1991. *Sourcebook of Health Insurance Data*. Health Insurance Association of America: Washington, D.C.

Heidenreich, Paul A., Mark B. McClellan, Craig Frances, and Laurence C. Baker. 2000. "Managed Care Market Share and Treatment of Myocardial Infarction for Fee-For-Service Medicare Patients." Working paper, Stanford University, Stanford, California.

Hellinger, Fred J. 1987. "Selection Bias in Health Maintenance Organizations: Analysis of Recent Evidence." *Health Care Financing Review* 9(2): 55–63.

_____. 1995. "Selection Bias in HMOs and PPOs: A Review of the Evidence." *Inquiry* 32(2): 135–142.

Hill, S.C., and B.L. Wolfe. 1997. "Testing the HMO Competitive Strategy: An Analysis of Its Impact on Medical Resources." *Journal of Health Economics* 16(3): 261–286.

Hoechst Marion Roussel. 1999. *HMO-PPO/Medicare-Medicaid Digest.* HMR Managed Care Digest Series, vol. 3. Wayne, New Jersey: Health Learning Systems.

Hosek, S.D., M. Susan Marquis, and K.B. Wells. 1990. *Health Care Utilization in Employer Plans with Preferred Provider Organization Options.* Santa Monica, California: RAND.

Interstudy. 1994. *Competitive Edge: HMO Industry Report.* Excelsior, Minnesota: Interstudy.

Kessler, D., and M. McClellan. 2000. "Is Hospital Competition Socially Wasteful?" *Quarterly Journal of Economics* 115(2): 577–617.

Langa, K.M., and E.J. Sussman. 1993. "The Effect of Cost-Containment Policies on Rates of Coronary Revascularization in California." *New England Journal of Medicine* 329(24): 1784–1789.

Luft, Harold S. 1981. *Health Maintenance Organizations: Dimensions of Performance.* New York: John Wiley and Sons.

Manning, Willard G., Arlene Leibowitz, G. Goldberg, W. Rogers, and Joseph Newhouse. 1984. "A Controlled Trial of the Effect of a Prepaid Group Practice on Use of Services." *New England Journal of Medicine* 310(23): 1505–1511.

McLaughlin, Catherine G. 1987. "HMO Growth and Hospital Expenses and Use: A Simultaneous-Equation Approach." *Health Services Research* 22(2): 183–205.

_____. 1988. "The Effect of HMOs on Overall Hospital Expenses: Is Anything Left after Correcting for Simultaneity and Selectivity?" *Health Services Research* 23(3): 421–441.

Miller, Robert H., and Harold S. Luft. 1994. "Managed Care Plan Performance since 1980. A Literature Analysis." *Journal of the American Medical Association* 271(19): 1512–1519.

_____. 1997. "Does Managed Care Lead to Better or Worse Quality of Care?" *Health Affairs* 16(5): 7–25.

Moy, E., A.J. Mazzaschi, R.J. Levin, D.A. Blake, and P.F. Griner. 1997. "Relationship between National Institutes of Health Research Awards to U.S. Medical Schools and Managed Care Market Penetration." *Journal of the American Medical Association* 278(3): 217–221.

Newhouse, Joseph P. 1992. "Medical Care Costs: How Much Welfare Loss?" *Journal of Economic Perspectives* 6(3): 3–21.

Noether, Monica. 1988. "Competition among Hospitals." *Journal of Health Economics* 7(3): 259–284.

Organisation for Economic Co-operation and Development. 1999. *OECD Health Data 1999: A Comparative Analysis of 29 Countries.* OECD, Paris.

Polsky, Daniel, Philip Kletke, Gregory Wozniak, and Jose Escarce. 2000. "HMO Penetration and the Geographic Mobility of Practicing Physicians." *Journal of Health Economics* 19(5): 793–809.

Robinson, James C. 1991. "HMO Market Penetration and Hospital Cost Inflation in California." *Journal of the American Medical Association* 266(19): 2719–2723.

_____. 1996. "Decline in Hospital Utilization and Cost Inflation under Managed Care in California." *Journal of the American Medical Association* 276(13): 1060–1064.

Rodgers, Jack, and Karen E. Smith. 1995. *Do Medicare HMOs Reduce Fee-For-Service Costs?* Washington, D.C: Price-Waterhouse LLP, Health Policy Economics Group.

Smith, D.G. 1997. "The Effects of Preferred Provider Organizations on Health Care Use and Costs." *Inquiry* 34(4): 278–287.

Ware, John E., Martha S. Bayliss, William H. Rogers, Mark Kosinski, and Alvin R. Tarlov. 1996. "Differences in 4-Year Health Outcomes for Elderly and Poor, Chronically Ill Patients Treated in HMO and Fee-For-Service Systems: Results from the Medical Outcomes Study." *Journal of the American Medical Association* 276(13): 1039–1047.

Weisbrod, Burton A., and C.L. LaMay. 1999. "Mixed Signals: Public Policy and the Future of Health Care R&D." *Health Affairs* 18(2): 112–125.

Welch, W. Pete. 1994. "HMO Market Share and Its Effect on Local Medicare Costs." In *HMOs and the Elderly*, Harold S. Luft, ed. Ann Arbor, Michigan: Health Administration Press, pp. 231–249.

Wickizer, Thomas M., and Paul J. Feldstein. 1995. "The Impact of HMO Competition on Private Health Insurance Premiums, 1985–1992." *Inquiry* 32(3): 241–251.

3

Covering the Uninsured

Incremental Policy Options
for the United States

Jonathan Gruber
Massachusetts Institute of Technology
and
National Bureau of Economic Research

The United States is alone among major industrialized nations in not having a universal guarantee of insurance coverage for its citizens. As a result, over 43 million Americans are currently uninsured, including over 10 million children. But this large uncovered population should not be taken to indicate that the U.S. government does not intervene in the market for health insurance to help those unable to obtain coverage. On the contrary, the single fastest growing federal entitlement program over the past decade is the Medicaid program, which provides health insurance coverage for low-income populations. In 1988, federal Medicaid expenditures were $54 billion; by 1998, expenditures had grown by almost 400 percent to $184 billion. But over this same period, the fraction of the non-elderly population without insurance coverage actually rose by almost 20 percent.[1]

The fact that this rapid growth in the Medicaid program has not checked the growth in the uninsured highlights the limitations of current public insurance policy as a means of guaranteeing universal access to the health care system. However, with universal coverage effectively erased from the policy horizon, partial solutions to the accessibility problem (such as the Medicaid program) are likely to be the alternative of choice for dealing with this problem in the near future. Indeed, since the failure of President Clinton's ambitious health insurance reform plan, government policy in this area has focused on incremental reforms. The two most important reforms of the past five years have been the expansion of public health insurance for children through the Children's Health Insurance Program (CHIP), and regulatory reforms of the private health insurance market through the Health Insurance Portability and Accountability Act (HIPAA). Recently, attention has turned to a third option—expanding tax subsidies for health insurance coverage.

In this chapter I will review the important health policy issues involved with different incremental routes to coverage of the uninsured in the United States. Then, after reviewing the facts about insurance coverage in the United States, I discuss what we have learned from the past 15 years of expansion of the Medicaid program, our traditional source of insurance coverage for indigent populations. The "Policy Directions" section contains a detailed analysis of the alternative directions that might be taken in expanding health insurance coverage in the United States: expanding the public insurance safety net up the income scale, filling in the gaps in the existing public insurance safety net, reforming the insurance market to increase access to private market policies, expanding limited mandates on employers, and using tax subsidies to induce expanded private coverage. The final section provides a brief summary.

INSURANCE COVERAGE IN THE UNITED STATES

While the elderly population is almost universally covered by the Medicare program, there are five primary insurance categories for the U.S. non-elderly population. These categories and how they have changed over time are shown in Table 1. The primary insurance category is coverage through the workplace, through which 64 percent of the non-elderly population obtain insurance coverage. Another 7 percent of the population obtains insurance coverage through other private insurance, primarily purchased in the nongroup insurance market. The primary remaining source of insurance coverage is the Medicaid program, which covers 11 percent of the non-elderly population; another 5 percent are covered by other sources of public insurance.

The final category is the uninsured. There are over 43 million uninsured, representing over 18 percent of the non-elderly population. Despite expansions in the Medicaid program, this figure has grown sig-

Table 1 Sources of Insurance Coverage for the Non-Elderly Population

Sources of coverage	1987		1997	
	Number (millions)	%	Number (millions)	%
Total private coverage	162.8	75.9	167.5	70.9
Employment-based	148.5	69.2	151.7	64.2
Own	72.5	33.8	77.4	32.8
Dependent	75.9	35.4	74.3	31.5
Other private	14.3	6.7	15.8	6.7
Medicare	11.6	5.4	11.3	4.8
Medicaid	18.4	8.6	26.0	11.0
No health insurance	31.8	14.8	43.1	18.3
Total near-elderly population	214.4	100	236.2	100

nificantly over the past decade because private insurance coverage has declined more rapidly than Medicaid has grown. It is this precipitous decline in employer-provided insurance coverage that provides the backdrop for thinking about new public efforts to cover the uninsured.

Who are the uninsured? Their characteristics are explored in Table 2. Almost 11 million of the uninsured are children. Importantly, the majority (almost 60 percent) of the uninsured are in families where the head of the family is a full-time, full-year worker, and another quarter are in families where there is part-time or part-year work. This fact has motivated continued efforts to increase insurance coverage through the expansion of employer-provided insurance. Interestingly, while the uninsured are poorer than average, they are not all poor; almost 40 percent of the uninsured have incomes over $30,000 per year. At the same time, the percentage of the income group that is uninsured falls sharply with income, from 43 percent under $5,000 of income to only 8 percent above $50,000 of income.

Why do we care if individuals are uninsured, more, say, than we are concerned about individuals simply being poor? Most directly, public concern about the uninsured derives from consideration of

Table 2 Characteristics of the Uninsured

Characteristic	Number (millions)	% of total uninsured	% within category
Total	43.1	100	100
Child	10.7	24.9	15.0
Adult worker	24.6	57.0	18.2
Adult nonworker	7.8	18.1	26.2
Family head is full-time, full-year	25.7	59.5	14.6
Family head is part-time/part-year	10.5	24.4	29.7
Family head is nonworker	6.9	16.1	28.4
Family income			
Under $5,000	5.0	11.6	42.8
$5,000–$9,999	3.8	8.7	28.8
$10,000–$14,999	5.4	12.4	37.0
$15,000–$19,999	4.7	10.8	32.6
$20,000–$29,999	7.7	17.9	26.6
$30,000–$39,999	5.1	11.8	18.2
$40,000–$49,999	3.7	8.5	14.4
$50,000 +	7.8	18.2	7.8

health insurance as a merit good, with intrinsic value beyond income. There is a general assumption that it is important for individuals to have insurance to maintain their health status. However, many economists emphasize that medical care may actually be of limited relevance for health, relative to the other behavioral and environmental factors that affect the health of low-income persons. So, an important and open question is whether providing more insurance coverage would actually improve the health of our population.

More indirectly, the uninsured impose real burdens, or "externalities," on those with insurance. This can occur most directly through communicable disease; if individuals without insurance forego vaccinations, for example, it can worsen the health of everyone. It can also occur indirectly, through financial channels. For example, hospitals pay over $15 billion dollars per year in "uncompensated care," primarily to the uninsured, for which they receive no reimbursement. Covering the uninsured would save these costs to the rest of society.

Finally, and potentially most importantly in economic terms, the prospect of becoming uninsured may have large productivity costs, as individuals with insurance are afraid to leave their jobs for fear of losing that insurance. This "job lock" has been shown to be a quantitatively important phenomenon by economists, with estimates that suggest that the fear of losing health insurance may lower mobility by as much as 25 percent. If individuals are locked into low-productivity positions with health insurance, it is a real loss in the value of output for the U.S. economy, and its financial implications may dwarf the $15 billion in uncompensated care noted above. More complete insurance coverage could alleviate this job lock.

MEDICAID POLICY

The primary public intervention in insurance markets for the non-elderly in the United States is the Medicaid program. At the outset, it is important to highlight that Medicaid is a program that serves three distinct populations: low-income women and children, the low-income disabled, and the low-income elderly, particularly nursing home residents. Spending is split roughly evenly between these three groups. In this chapter, I will focus on the first of these groups, women and children, since I am concentrating on health insurance coverage, and the elderly and the disabled are primarily covered by the Medicare program for their medical expenditures.

Historically, Medicaid eligibility for women and children has been tied to participation in the Aid for Families with Dependent Children program (AFDC). This linkage with AFDC restricted access to the program to low-income single mothers, in some cases very low income. For example, the income cutoff for eligibility for a family of four in South Carolina in 1984 was only 29 percent of the poverty line. Beginning in 1984, and particularly after 1987, the program began to expand eligibility for all children and pregnant women; that is, these expansions applied only to the expenses of pregnancy for women. By

1992, states were required to cover all pregnant women and children under the age of six up to 133 percent of poverty (independent of family composition), and were allowed to expand coverage up to 185 percent of poverty. In addition, children born after September 30, 1983, were mandatorily covered up to 100 percent of poverty (once again independent of family composition).

On top of these federal mandates was a host of state actions to expand coverage, both at a faster pace and to a broader range of children than is provided for by federal legislation. For example, children in Texas saw a 28 percentage-point increase in their eligibility for Medicaid between 1984 and 1992, while eligibility for children in Wisconsin actually declined by 4 percent (Gruber 1997).

How Does Medicaid Affect Health?

Ultimately, the question of interest for policymakers is how these policy changes impacted the health of the low-income population, and at what cost. To understand the effects of Medicaid policy on health, however, it is important to trace through the channels by which changes at the legislative level are translated to actual health improvements.

The process by which Medicaid determines health is depicted in Figure 1. The first step in evaluating the effect of Medicaid policy changes on outcomes of interest, such as health, is to examine the effects on the eligibility of persons for the Medicaid program. The next step is the translation of Medicaid eligibility into Medicaid coverage. An important general feature of social insurance programs is that individuals do not always take up the benefits for which they are eligible. Previous research has found that only about two-thirds of those eligible for the unemployment insurance, AFDC, and food stamps programs take up their benefits.[2]

The previously uninsured are not the only group that takes up benefits, however. In fact, two-thirds of those made eligible for the expansions actually had private insurance already. Some of those individuals will find it attractive to drop that private insurance and join the Medicaid program. Along some dimensions, Medicaid is a much more generous plan than most private policies, since it has no co-payments, covers prescription drugs, and often covers optional services such as

Figure 1 Medicaid Eligibility Policy

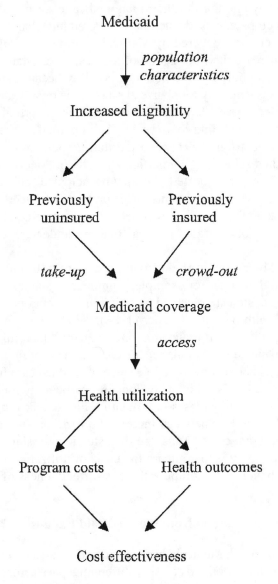

SOURCE: Gruber (2000).

dental care. In contrast, under the typical private insurance policy, individuals pay one-third of their total medical costs out of pocket, in the form of co-payments, deductibles, and premium-sharing.

Moreover, once covered by Medicaid, individuals will not automatically increase their utilization of medical care. Many physicians do not treat publicly insured patients, possibly because public insurance programs generally reimburse at rates far below private fee levels. A number of observers have alleged that there is a shortfall in the supply of physicians willing to serve Medicaid patients. The American Medical Association (1991) reported that 26 percent of physicians described themselves as "nonparticipants" in the Medicaid program, and only 34 percent reported that they participated "fully" and were accepting new Medicaid patients. This problem is exacerbated by the fact that many of the patients who would be made eligible for public insurance are concentrated in areas that are underserved by physicians.[3]

Finally, increases in the utilization of care will not necessarily improve child health—for example, a number of studies suggest that much of the acute care received by children is inappropriate and may have little health benefit. Kemper (1988), for example, found that 21 percent of pediatric hospitalization days were of "doubtful necessity," and that this percentage is higher for insured than for uninsured children. And, as noted above, the relevance of medical care for health is not yet firmly established in many domains, particularly for children.

Whether or not increases in utilization improve health outcomes, there is a definite link between increased utilization and increases in Medicaid program costs. Thus, the final step in assessing the efficacy of Medicaid policy is to compare the costs of utilization increases to any health benefits, to compute the cost-effectiveness of eligibility increases.

What Have We Learned from the Medicaid Expansions?

As I have noted, Medicaid has expanded dramatically over the past 15 years, and it has done so at a very differential pace across the United States. This variation across the states has provided a "natural laboratory" for studying the impacts of Medicaid on insurance coverage, health utilization, and health outcomes. A large number of studies have examined the various links in Figure 1, with several important conclusions.

First, the Medicaid expansions tremendously increased the eligibility of low-income women and children for health insurance coverage. Figure 2 shows the growth in eligibility for health insurance coverage under Medicaid for children and for pregnant women. For both groups, there is a gradual increase in eligibility from 1984 through 1987, and a much more rapid increase thereafter; these correspond to the two eras denoted above. By 1992, almost one-half of all women were eligible for Medicaid for the expenses of pregnancy, and almost one-third of children aged 0–14 were eligible for all of their medical spending.

Second, the rate at which this new Medicaid eligibility was translated to new Medicaid coverage is quite low. Estimates of the take-up rate, or the increase in coverage among those made eligible, are approximately 25 percent, suggesting that three-quarters of those made eligible by the expansions did not take up coverage. This fact is confirmed by Figure 3, which shows time-series data on coverage for children and women of child-bearing age. While both series rise steeply, the increase is much less than that of eligibility; moreover, much of the rise after 1989 is due to the recession, not eligibility policy.

Third, one reason for this low take-up is that two-thirds of those made eligible for the expansions already had private health insurance coverage. The fact that such a large share of the newly eligible population under the Medicaid expansions had access to private insurance raises the prospect that many of the new enrollees on the program may have been "crowded out" of private insurance purchases. The time-series evidence on insurance coverage in the United States would seem to confirm the crowd-out hypothesis; there is a remarkable time-series correlation between Medicaid coverage and private insurance coverage over this period.

A number of careful econometric studies have considered the magnitude of crowd-out, in terms of the change in private insurance coverage due to Medicaid policy, relative to the increase in the Medicaid rolls.[4] Virtually all of these studies have concluded that crowd-out is significant, with estimates as high as 50 percent; that is, for every two persons who joined the Medicaid rolls, one person is losing private health insurance.

Figure 2 Medicaid Eligibility of Women and Children

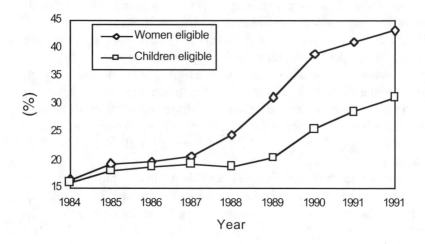

Figure 3 Medicaid Coverage of Women and Children

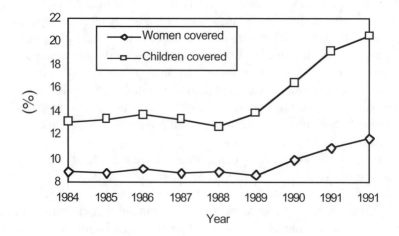

Fourth, despite the fact that only some of those joining Medicaid were formerly uninsured, there is a noticeable improvement in utilization of health services. Studies have found significant increases in utilization of first trimester prenatal care by mothers who became eligible for Medicaid, and in the utilization of preventive physician visits by children who became eligible (Currie and Gruber 1996a,b). For example, Currie and Gruber found that children made eligible for Medicaid saw a 50 percent reduction in the likelihood of going a full year without a doctor's visit.

Fifth, these increases in utilization were translated to improved health. The primary focus of studies in this area has been on mortality, which is an easily measured and interpreted, albeit extreme, measure of health. Studies have found that the expansions of Medicaid led to an 8.5 percent decline in infant mortality, and a 5.1 percent decline in child mortality (Currie and Gruber 1996a,b). These are significant effects.

Finally, these expansions did significantly increase the costs of the Medicaid program, as would be expected given increased enrollment and utilization. Given the impact on infant mortality, and the associated increased costs, the expansions were associated with a cost on the order of $2 million per life saved. Is this figure large or small? Relative to the promised cost savings by those who advocate increased insurance and preventive care, this figure is quite large. However, relative to either the economics literature on individual revelations of the value of their life through choices (such as purchases of safety equipment or taking risky jobs, which implies a value of $4–$7 million) or to the cost per life saved through other government programs (such as safety regulations for cars and busses, which can cost upwards of $1 billion per life saved) this seems like a reasonable investment.

POLICY DIRECTIONS

Given the failure of the Medicaid expansions to check the growth of the uninsured in the United States, there is considerable interest in alternative policy directions for expanding insurance coverage. The major attempted reform of recent years was the Health Security Act

(HSA) initiative of the Clinton Administration in 1994, which proposed through employer mandate and expanded public subsidies to move toward universal coverage of the population. In the wake of the spectacular defeat of this effort, more incremental reforms have proceeded in recent years, at both the federal and state level. In this section, I will review alternative approaches to this problem, and consider their pros and cons from a health economics perspective.

Guiding Principle: Efficiency

When thinking about policy alternatives, it is important to recognize that any new spending on insurance expansions will be limited in the current budgetary climate. That makes it critical to focus on the efficiency of new spending, or the bang-for-the-buck. That is, for any program, it is imperative to consider how many individuals will gain insurance coverage on net, relative to the amount spent. The crowd-out discussion in the previous section points out that this is not a trivial issue. The more that public dollars are spent on populations that already have insurance, the more that the take-up of these public programs is likely to be among those who already have insurance.

At the same time, the bulk of the uninsured reside in working, lower-middle income households, and the vast majority of these households do have health insurance. So if serious inroads are to be made on the uninsured, the issue of crowd-out cannot be avoided and must be addressed head-on. This suggests that policy be designed in a manner that minimizes the appeal of any public subsidies to those who already have health insurance, while still making the program attractive to those who don't.

Further Expansions of Public Insurance up the Income Scale

One straightforward alternative for increasing insurance coverage is to continue to expand our public insurance safety net. This was the approach taken by the recent Children's Health Insurance Program (CHIP), enacted by Congress as part of the Balanced Budget Act of 1997. This program provides roughly $5 billion per year in matching funds for states to expand health insurance coverage for children beyond the eligibility provided for by existing Medicaid programs.

States can use these funds to either expand the traditional Medicaid program or to create a new program that meets certain criteria but is more flexible than Medicaid along some dimensions. For example, under alternative programs there is more flexibility about the benefits package covered and more freedom to charge premiums and co-payments to enrollees. Initially, many states have focused on Medicaid expansions, but more and more appear to be turning to alternative program structures to circumvent some of the restrictions of the Medicaid program.

The problem with this approach is that the CHIP program will be spending its dollars primarily on those children around 200 percent of poverty, a population that is already heavily privately insured. For example, among those children between 200 and 250 percent of poverty, only 14 percent are uninsured and almost 80 percent already have private health insurance. This raises the prospect of significant crowd-out with the CHIP expansions, and little new coverage as a result.

On the other hand, the flexibilities built into CHIP are likely to help mitigate crowd-out. By making the benefits package less generous than Medicaid, and by introducing premiums and co-payments for services, state CHIP programs make it less attractive to drop one's private health insurance to join the public program. Clearly, as public insurance is expanded further and further up the income scale, given the strong correlation between income and private insurance coverage, more and more limitation of this form is called for.

An important priority for research is to assess whether the flexibilities in CHIP have a real impact on crowd-out. Some causal evidence suggests that they might. Two states that introduced nontrivial premiums into their Medicaid programs (Minnesota and Florida) have seen relatively low levels of crowd-out, less than 10 percent in each case. While this evidence is only suggestive, it does highlight the potential importance of making the program less attractive as it is expanded up the income scale.

Outreach

While expansions of insurance up the income scale seems an obvious way to reach more uninsured, the CHIP legislation largely ignored a needier and more obvious population: those who are already eligible for Medicaid but don't take it up. Indeed, most estimates suggest that there are on the order of four million children who are eligible for Medicaid but don't take up coverage. Moreover, while most women who are eligible for coverage of birthing expenses are signed up for that coverage by hospitals, there is tremendous underuse of prenatal care services by women who are eligible for Medicaid but don't use it to cover those services. The reasons for this limited take-up are unclear and reflect some mix of poor information about eligibility and stigma about enrollment in a public insurance program.

Regardless of the cause, however, this is a very high bang-for-the-buck population. Of those children not on Medicaid already but with incomes below 150 percent of the poverty line, 53 percent are uninsured. This suggests that the highest priority for government policy is to expand coverage of this group through outreach initiatives, even if they are somewhat costly. In other words, in thinking about expanding insurance coverage in the low-income population, it is probably best to think about filling the cup from the bottom: start by maximizing the coverage of the lowest-income population with few other insurance alternatives, and then move to higher-income groups that often have access to private coverage.

Other Demographic Groups

For largely political reasons, the expansions of health insurance through both Medicaid and CHIP have focused on children and pregnant women. Yet there is little coherent argument for covering an 18-year-old woman up to 200 percent of poverty, while a 19-year-old woman receives no public coverage unless she is pregnant or on welfare. This is particularly true given the low use of prenatal care by lower-income women; if they had continuous insurance coverage, they would perhaps be more likely to seek care as soon as they got pregnant.

One particularly helpful proposal that has been discussed is to extend coverage to the parents of Medicaid and CHIP children. This would have the additional advantage of increasing take-up by the children, because once the parents are eligible it might increase their awareness of the entire family's entitlement.

Insurance Market Reforms

The problem with any public insurance expansion in today's budgetary climate is that funding is likely to be extremely limited. As a result, much attention has been paid to insurance market reforms as a means of expanding coverage. The Health Insurance Portability and Accountability Act (HIPAA) attempted to address one perceived cause of uninsurance in the United States, which was practices of private insurers that made the individual insurance market an unattractive place to purchase insurance. In particular, this bill mandated that private insurers permit the conversion of group policies to individual coverage, so that high-cost individuals who were leaving their jobs could continue to access insurance. It also set limits on the applicability of preexisting conditions exclusions, and it guaranteed that small groups who applied for insurance would be offered coverage.

In principle, these types of reforms are an alternative means of expanding coverage with little public cost. However, while the evidence thus far is limited, it suggests that these reforms have had little effect, primarily because insurers have an easy means of circumventing these restrictions: raising prices, which are not federally regulated.

At the same time, a number of states have been passing similar and often more expansive private insurance market regulations. In addition to the types of features noted above, states are experimenting with price regulation that is designed to deal with the primary problem facing HIPAA, primarily for small firms and to a lesser extent for individuals. A number of states have mandated that prices stay within certain bands, so that the highest-cost firm or individual cannot be charged more than the lowest-cost firm or individual. Some states have even gone so far as to mandate community rating, whereby all firms or individuals in certain categories must be charged the same price.

The evidence on the impact of these state regulations is once again limited. But one recent provocative study suggests that these policies have increased access for the most costly populations at the expense of the least costly: insurance coverage has risen for older and higher-cost workers but has fallen more for younger and lower-cost workers, for a net reduction in insurance coverage. This would be consistent with an insurer reaction to these regulations of raising all premiums while making them uniform, in order to ensure the profitability of insurance.

Thus, the experience of both HIPAA and state regulations suggests the substantial limits of insurance market reform as a mechanism for expanding insurance coverage. While the evidence thus far is limited, there is certainly no suggestion that these reforms are dramatically, or even modestly, increasing insurance coverage, and they may in fact be having perverse effects on coverage.

Mandates

Another route of somewhat limited public intervention is targeted mandates on employers, at a level much more modest than the major mandates envisioned by the Health Security Act. The most important existing federal and state mandates on employers related to insurance coverage are the "continuation of coverage" mandates that were passed by a number of states starting in the 1970s, and then by the federal government in 1986. These laws stipulate that employers must allow their employees to continue to purchase insurance at group prices, which are generally much lower than nongroup costs, for a period of time (18 months by federal law) after leaving a job. This is a valuable benefit for employees who are losing jobs or moving to new positions without health insurance, as it allows them to tap into the much more efficient group market rather than face the high prices and often discriminatory practices of the individual insurance market.

A number of studies have suggested that these types of continuation policies have been a success in raising insurance coverage significantly among job leavers, particularly among those who don't move immediately into a new job with insurance. These studies have found that continuation coverage also had the collateral benefit of loosening "job lock" by allowing individuals a source of modestly priced coverage when they wanted to move from low- to high-productivity positions. Moreover, there is no evidence that these mandates have been particularly onerous to employers; for example, there has been no effect of the mandates on employers' propensity to offer insurance.

These studies suggest that there could be value in further extending continuation coverage; for example, by subsidizing the costs of group policies for those leaving their jobs, and by making this insurance available for a longer period of time.

Tax Policy

The final type of alternative to be considered is tax subsidies. Currently, health insurance purchases are subsidized for two groups: employees and the self-employed. Employee costs are subsidized through the exclusion of employer-paid health insurance premiums (and some employee-paid premiums as well) from an individual's taxable income. This subsidy is currently estimated to cost over $100 billion per year in foregone revenues to the federal government (Sheils and Hogan 1999). The costs of the self-employed have been partially subsidized since 1986; currently 60 percent of the health insurance costs of the self-employed can be deducted from taxable income, and this share will rise to 100 percent by 2003 (Meyer, Silow-Carroll, and Wicks 1999).

This system of tax subsidies leaves three groups without tax subsidies for the purchase of health insurance:

- those who work for firms that do not offer health insurance,
- those who are not employees nor self-employed, such as the unemployed or early retirees (before the age of Medicare eligibility), and
- those who work for firms that do not offer a Section 125 plan (i.e., a "cafeteria plan") that allows employees to contribute the employees' share of health insurance premiums on a pretax basis.

Each of these holes represents a significant population. Roughly 15 percent of the non-elderly population is at a point in time not eligible for a tax subsidy to health insurance, and roughly 21 percent of insurance spending among those who are insured is not tax subsidized.[5]

As a result, a string of recent proposals have considered expanding in one way or another the tax deductibility of health insurance. In its most ambitious form, some of these proposals would end the employer tax exclusion and introduce unlimited individual tax exclusions in its place. However, most of the proposed legislation in this area has suggested more limited (although still potentially quite costly) interventions, usually in the form of limited credits or deductions toward the purchase of health insurance. Even within this framework, however, there is considerable variation in the details of the policies proposed, along dimensions such as the generosity of the credit, the income ranges to which it would apply, and the potential pool of people eligible.

I have built a detailed simulation model to analyze the impact of tax policy alternatives (Gruber 2000), and there are two important lessons from this analysis for using tax policy to cover the uninsured. First, even expansive tax policies cannot cover a very sizeable fraction of the uninsured. For example, I estimate that a policy that provided a $2,000 credit for single persons and a $4,000 credit for families for the purchase of nongroup insurance will cost almost $35 billion dollars per year, a sum that almost certainly exceeds congressional willingness to spend money to address this issue but would cover only about 5.5 million uninsured, or less than one-seventh of the uninsured population.

Second, there is an inverse relationship between the generosity of policies and their efficiency. For example, a credit that is one-quarter as generous as that described above would cost only $1.4 billion per year, and would cover almost one million uninsured. This is a cost of only $1,550 per person who gains insurance, compared to a cost of over $6,200 per person who gains insurance with the more expansive credit. This is because as the credit is made more generous, targeting is worse. More generous credits are taken up extensively by both those who already have nongroup insurance, so that we are just paying their costs, or those who have group insurance and are paying some costs, and so would rather switch to highly subsidized nongroup insurance (a crowd-out-type effect). Thus, we see the same problem that we saw with public insurance expansions: as policy attempts to get more generous, it faces larger crowd-out problems and declining efficiency of public spending.

CONCLUSIONS—WHERE DO WE GO?

The sizeable growth of the uninsured population in the face of the robust economy of the past six years is striking and disturbing. It suggests that we cannot count on standard economic forces to simply solve this problem, and that serious reductions in the number of uninsured may require more dramatic government intervention. The experience of the Medicaid expansions suggests that government intervention can work to improve the health of low-income populations, but that as this intervention is expanded farther, the cost of further reductions in the uninsured population may be quite steep.

It seems clear that the first policies the government should pursue are bottom-of-the-cup policies that target those groups which generally have little other recourse to insurance. One clear group in this category is the up to seven million children currently eligible for, but not enrolled in, public insurance. Another such group may be very low-income adults who have been excluded from the dramatic increases in insurance eligibility of the past decade and a half. These are groups that are primarily uninsured and for which the bang-for-the-buck would be highest for new government health insurance expenditures.

Beyond this, society must recognize the high costs of additional reductions in the number of uninsured. These costs can be minimized through public insurance expansions, which are relatively unattractive to those with private insurance today, such as by adding premiums or restricting benefits. Tax policy remains a viable option, but it is difficult to design a tax policy that has a very large impact at a modest cost. Tax subsidies are likely to be most useful as part of a larger package, rather than as a stand-alone solution.

In conclusion, the economics profession has a lot to add to the debate over health insurance coverage. We have provided clear evidence that health insurance coverage expansions can improve health, but that costs can be high due to insurance crowd-out. And economic principles of efficiency deliver a quite clear message for the first priorities for new public spending on health insurance coverage: start with the groups that are most in need of insurance coverage. If policymakers heed these lessons, we can efficiently move toward reducing the burden of uninsurance in the United States today.

Notes

1. Data on Medicaid spending from U.S. Congress Committee on Ways and Means (1998); data on insurance coverage from Employee Benefit Research Institute (1999).
2. Blank and Card (1991) estimated that takeup of unemployment insurance benefits only about two-thirds, and Blank and Ruggles (1996) estimated similar takeup for AFDC and food stamps.

3. For example, Fossett et al. (1992) compared Chicago neighborhoods with 50 per-cent of the population on welfare to neighborhoods with 10 percent of the popula-tion on welfare and found that there were twice as many physicians practicing in the wealthier areas (on a per child basis).
4. See, for example, Cutler and Gruber (1996) Dubay and Kenney (1997), Blum-berg, Dubay, and Norton (2000), and Rask and Rask (2000).
5. Author's tabulations from the March 1997 Current Population Survey.

References

American Medical Association. 1991. *Physician Marketplace Update, July 1991.* AMA: Chicago, Illinois.

Blank, Rebecca, and David Card. 1991. "Recent Trends in Insured and Unin-sured Unemployment: Is There an Explanation?" *Quarterly Journal of Economics* 106(4): 1157–1190.

Blank, Rebecca, and Patricia Ruggles. 1996. "When Do Women Use AFDC and Food Stamps? The Dynamics of Eligibility versus Participation." *Journal of Human Resources* 31(1): 57–89.

Blumberg, Linda, Lisa Dubay, and Stephen Norton. 2000. "Did the Medicaid Expansions for Children Displace Private Insurance? An Analysis Using the SIPP." *Journal of Health Economics* 19(1): 33–61.

Currie, Janet, and Jonathan Gruber. 1996a. "Saving Babies: The Efficacy and Cost of Recent Changes in the Medicaid Eligibility for Pregnant Women." *Journal of Political Economy* 104(6): 1263–1296.

———. 1996b. "Health Insurance Eligibility, Utilization of Medical Care, and Child Health." *Quarterly Journal of Economics* 111(2): 431–466.

Cutler, David, and Jonathan Gruber. 1996. "Does Public Insurance Crowd Out Private Insurance?" *Quarterly Journal of Economics* 111(2): 391–430.

Dubay, Lisa, and Genevieve Kenney. 1997. "Did Medicaid Expansions for Pregnant Women Crowd Out Private Insurance?" *Health Affairs* 16(1): 185–193.

Employee Benefit Research Institute. 1999. *Sources of Health Insurance and Characteristics of the Uninsured.* Washington, D.C.: EBRI.

Fossett, James W., Janet D. Perloff, Phillip R. Kletke, and John A. Peterson. 1992. "Medicaid and Access to Child Health Care in Chicago." *Journal of Health Politics, Policy and Law* 17: 273–298.

Gruber, Jonathan. 1997. "Health Insurance for Poor Women and Children in the U.S.: Lessons from the Past Decade." In *Tax Policy and the Economy*

11, James Poterba, ed. Cambridge, Massachusetts: MIT Press, pp. 169–211.

_____. 2000. "Health Insurance and the Labor Market." In *The Handbook of Health Economics*, Joseph Newhouse and Anthony Culyer, eds. Amsterdam: North-Holland, pp. 645–706.

Kemper, Kathi. 1988. "Medically Inappropriate Hospital Use in a Pediatric Population." *The New England Journal of Medicine* 243: 1033–1037.

Meyer, Jack, Sharon Silow-Carroll, and Elliot Wicks. 1999. "Tax Reform to Expand Health Coverage: Administrative Issues and Challenges." Report prepared for the Kaiser Family Foundation.

Rask, Kevin, and Kimberly Rask. 2000. "Public Insurance Substituting for Private Insurance: New Evidence Regarding Public Hospitals, Uncompensated Care Funds, and Medicaid." *Journal of Health Economics* 19(1): 1–32.

Sheils, John, and Paul Hogan. 1999. "Cost of Tax-Exempt Health Benefits in 1998." *Health Affairs* 18(2): 176–181.

U.S. Congress, Committee on Ways and Means. 1998. *Green Book 1998: Background Material on Programs under the Jurisdiction of the Committee on Ways and Means*, Washington D.C.: GPO.

4

Health Insurance
and the Labor Market

Brigitte Madrian
University of Chicago

The system of health insurance and health care delivery in the United States is very much like a patchwork quilt, one pieced together from scraps of cloth of different shapes, sizes, patterns, and textures, and colors. Like the quilt, we have a patchworked array of insurance-providing institutions in the United States, each covering a different segment of the population, and each with its own idiosyncratic rules—its differences in shape, size, pattern, texture, and color, if you will.

There are

- the Medicare part A and B pieces that cover those over age 65 and the disabled under age 65;

- the Medigap pieces that provide additional coverage to the elderly, beyond that available through Medicare;

- the various state Medicaid pieces covering those who are or who have recently been on welfare, or those whose incomes are sufficiently low;

- the myriad of employment-related health insurance pieces, covering many but not all employees, along with their spouses and dependents;

- the employment-based retiree health insurance pieces, covering the former employees of companies, those who have since retired; and

- the pieces that cover students attending various universities throughout the country and elsewhere.

And then there is the backdrop, the part of the quilt that generally goes unnoticed: the uninsured individuals who are not covered by any of the other insurance pieces and who must pay for their medical expenditures out of pocket or receive uncompensated care.

The analogy can only be taken so far, however. The patchwork quilt evokes images of warmth, love, home and hearth, hot cocoa, a crackling fire at a cabin in the woods. In contrast, the patchwork U.S. health insurance system is more likely to evoke images of frustration, hassle, red tape, paperwork, and annoying voice-automated telephone response systems. The patchwork quilt is not a perfect metaphor, but it is a good one.

There are many important economic implications associated with the fragmented, patchwork system of health insurance coverage that we have in the United States. This chapter focuses on one of these economic implications, namely, the relationship between the various institutions that provide health insurance in the United States, and the labor market decisions made by individuals and employers. More than two-thirds of the gross domestic product in the United States is derived from the labor market—the labor services of individuals employed in producing goods and services in the economy. Distortions in the efficient operation of the labor market can thus have a tremendous effect not only on the welfare of specific individuals, but on the economy as a whole.

But what is the link between health insurance and the labor market? Why is this even a concern? The link derives from the characteristics of the pieces in the patchwork quilt. Many of the insurance-providing institutions in the United States, the pieces of the patchwork quilt, have some connection, either directly or indirectly, to the employment status of individuals. The idiosyncratic relationships between the labor market and the types of health insurance coverage that are available to individuals affects the labor market behavior of both individuals and firms in some very interesting and economically important ways.

Before analyzing the labor market effects of health insurance in the United States, it is important to more closely examine the pieces of the quilt—the various health insurance institutions—and how they are tied to the labor market.

HEALTH INSURANCE INSTITUTIONS
IN THE UNITED STATES

By far the most significant piece of the quilt, at least in terms of magnitude, is employer-provided health insurance coverage. This employee benefit provides health insurance to 64 percent of the non-elderly U.S. population. Some of these individuals, about half, receive this coverage by virtue of their own employment, while the rest receive it as dependents of a spouse or parent who works. In addition, some employers provide so-called "retiree" health insurance to former employees who have retired. About 45 percent of the elderly have this type of health insurance from a previous employer.

It is interesting to consider why the United States, in contrast to most other developed countries, has a health insurance system in which employers are the primary providers of insurance rather than the government, at least for the non-elderly, and also why employers are the primary providers of health insurance but not other types of insurance. The United States has repeatedly rejected broad attempts to "socialize" either medical care or health insurance provision. The first such initiative, during the 1930s, failed despite the concurrent genesis of so many other New Deal government social programs. The most recent initiative was the failed Clinton administration attempt at national health reform. And there have been other similarly doomed attempts in the interim. In the absence of universal government-provided health insurance coverage, market forces have pushed employers into their role as primary providers of insurance. These market forces include

- a substantial price advantage given to employers through the tax code because firm health insurance expenditures on behalf of their employees are not counted as taxable income to either the firm or the employees,

- economies of scale that derive from providing health insurance to a large group of individuals, and

- the effectiveness of the workplace as a pooling mechanism to overcome the problems of adverse selection that plague some individual insurance markets, especially the individual market for health insurance.

As an institution, employer-provided health was really established during the two decades following World War II, although there are some limited examples of employers providing such coverage before the war.

The second, third, and fourth pieces of the quilt are various types of government-sponsored health insurance: Medicare, Medicaid, and CHAMPUS. It is interesting that even at the governmental level, there is no single unified health insurance program. By far the largest government health insurance program is Medicare. Medicare was implemented in 1965 to provide health insurance coverage to the elderly, individuals aged 65 and over, many of whom were left uninsured or underinsured upon their retirement when coverage through their former employers ceased. Medicare also covers some individuals under age 65, specifically those who are disabled and eligible for Social Security Disability Insurance. Currently, Medicare covers over 96 percent of those over age 65, and 5 percent of those under age 65.

The third piece of the quilt, Medicaid, is a state-run program funded jointly by the state and federal governments. This program was traditionally a health insurance program for welfare recipients, primarily single mothers and their children, and also for the low-income elderly. In recent years it has been expanded to provide coverage to non-welfare-eligible families with modest incomes, particularly children. There is great heterogeneity among states in the eligibility requirements for Medicaid, and in the benefits that are actually provided—yet another example of the fragmented, patchwork nature of U.S. health insurance. Overall, 9 percent of the elderly are covered by Medicaid, as are 11 percent of the non-elderly.

The fourth governmentally provided piece of the quilt is CHAMPUS/VA, the program that provides health insurance to members of the uniformed services and their families, and to veterans. About 3 percent of the population is covered by this type of health insurance, a fraction that has been falling steadily for years as the number of those in active military service declines because of military cutbacks, and as the number of veterans declines.

The final piece of the patchwork quilt is a bit of a catchall—other private insurance. This category encompasses a broad array of institutions ranging from supplemental Medigap coverage for the elderly, to university-provided health insurance for students, to individually purchased policies from traditional insurers such as Blue Cross/Blue

Shield, to health insurance provided through membership organizations such as a credit union or a trade or professional association. Together, these various types of other private insurance cover about 7 percent of the non-elderly population, and perhaps as much as one-third of the elderly population.

Then, of course, there are the uninsured, those who do not have health insurance through their own or a family member's employment, who are not old enough or disabled enough to qualify for Medicare, who are not eligible or decline to participate in Medicaid or CHAMPUS/VA, and who either cannot afford or choose not to purchase health insurance in the private market. These 43 million individuals represent about 18 percent of the non-elderly population. Due in large part to Medicare, only a small fraction of the elderly, about 1 percent, are uninsured.

With this brief introduction to the various "pieces" of the insurance quilt, let us now turn to how this patchwork array of insurance institutions affects the labor market decisions made by individuals and firms.

HEALTH INSURANCE AND RETIREMENT

Perhaps the most important labor market outcome to consider is employment itself—how does health insurance affect individual participation in the labor market? It affects participation because certain types of health insurance are provided as a condition of employment (for example, employer-provided health insurance), while other types of health insurance are more readily available when individuals are not employed, or not fully employed (for example, Medicaid or university-sponsored student health insurance), while still others are available regardless of employment status (for example, Medicare for those over age 65).

With respect to the effects of health insurance, the most widely studied facet of labor force participation that has been examined is retirement. To what extent does health insurance determine when and how individuals choose to withdraw from the labor force? The answer lies in the interaction between three different pieces of the patchwork quilt: employer-provided health insurance for active employees, employer-provided retiree health insurance, and Medicare. As already noted, many but not all employers provide health insurance to their employees and to their spouses and dependents. This insurance, however, is usually conditional on employment; employees who cease to work usually find that their health insurance coverage ceases as well. Some companies, however, offer retiree health insurance. About one-third of employers continue to provide health insurance to some or all of their former employees who have retired. For individuals who work at these companies and who are eligible for retiree health insurance, retirement does not imply a loss of health insurance coverage. And once individuals reach age 65, even the absence of retiree health insurance does not imply a loss of health insurance coverage upon retirement, because virtually everyone aged 65 and older is eligible for Medicare.

The interactions between these three different types of health insurance provide several venues through which health insurance can affect the retirement behavior of older individuals. For example, some individuals work in firms that provide retiree health insurance while others do not. For individuals who are younger than 65 and not yet eligible for Medicare, a lack of retiree health insurance should serve as a deterrent to retirement, at least until individuals reach the age of 65. Several studies have found consistent evidence that individuals whose employers provide retiree health insurance leave the labor force earlier than individuals whose employers do not (Madrian 1994a; Karoly and Rogowski 1994; Gustman and Steinmeier 1994; Rust and Phelan 1997; Blau and Gilleskie 1997; and Rogowski and Karoly 2000). My own research suggests that individuals with access to retiree health insurance leave the labor market between 6 and 18 months earlier than individuals who do not have access to retiree health insurance (Madrian 1994a). These individuals are also much more likely to retire before the age of 65. Evidence along these lines but of a more anecdotal nature also comes from a recent Gallup poll in which "61 percent of workers reported that they would not retire before becoming eligible for Medicare if their employer did not provide retiree health benefits." (Employee Benefit Research Institute 1993).

The key thing that generates the relationship between health insurance and retirement just described is that retiree health insurance essentially makes employer-provided health insurance portable across the transition from work to retirement. Individuals with other types of portable or quasi-portable health insurance should also be more likely to retire, at least before the age of 65, than individuals without portable health insurance. Another institution that makes employer-provided health insurance at least somewhat portable is COBRA, a federal law that took effect in 1986 that requires employers to allow former employees to buy into their former employers' health insurance plan for up to 18 months. In terms of motivating retirement, COBRA is not as generous as retiree health insurance for two reasons: it is of only limited duration while retiree health insurance is not, and it requires much greater out-of-pocket payments than does retiree health insurance. Nevertheless, there is also evidence that the limited health insurance portability instituted through COBRA increased retirement rates for those under age 65 by almost 30 percent (Gruber and Madrian 1995).

Individuals who are covered by non-employment-based health insurance (for example, through Medicaid or policies purchased individually in the private market) also have a type of health insurance coverage that is portable across the transition from work to retirement. Once again, empirical evidence suggests that these individuals are also more likely to retire than are individuals with employer-provided health insurance that would be lost upon retirement, at least before the age of 65 (Rust and Phelan 1997).

An interesting thing happens at age 65 when individuals become eligible for Medicare: even for those individuals with employer-provided health insurance that does not continue into retirement, leaving the labor force no longer implies a loss of health insurance because individuals are covered by Medicare. Thus, Medicare eligibility should provide a strong retirement incentive for those individuals not eligible for retiree health insurance. And indeed, a substantial fraction of 64-year-olds do retire at age 65 when they become eligible for Medicare. Empirical research has to date been unable to precisely quantify the magnitude of this Medicare-induced retirement effect because age 65 also happens to be the normal age to qualify for Social Security and the age at which many pension plans provide full retirement benefits. With so many other factors motivating retirement that are coincident with Medicare eligibility, it is difficult to quantify exactly how big each of the respective effects are. But the evidence on how other types of health insurance affect retirement suggests that Medicare eligibility should be very important as well.

One idiosyncratic feature of Medicare, which, like other types of health insurance, also generates interesting variations in retirement behavior, is that Medicare only covers individuals and not spouses or dependent children. As a result, the retirement decisions of two individuals without retiree health insurance who are both about to turn 65, one with a spouse who is younger and the other with a spouse who is older, could be quite different. For the individual with the older spouse, retirement at the age of Medicare eligibility will result in a loss of health insurance coverage for neither spouse—both will be covered by Medicare. Indeed, the older spouse already is. In contrast, retirement at the age of Medicare eligibility for the individual with a younger spouse will result in a loss of health insurance coverage for the spouse if the spouse was covered as a dependent on the employee's plan and not through his or her own independent coverage. Interestingly, men with younger wives are less likely to retire than are men with older wives until their spouses also become eligible for Medicare (Madrian and Beaulieu 1998). Thus, retirement is affected not only by one's own Medicare eligibility, but also by the Medicare eligibility of one's spouse.

Health insurance also affects the nature of the transition from work to retirement. Some individuals move from full-time work to full-time retirement, while others pursue a more gradual transition from work to retirement, moving from full-time work to part-time work, and then eventually to full-time retirement. Because employer-provided health insurance is typically contingent upon full-time employment, it is usually difficult to maintain employer-provided health insurance while working part-time. Individuals with retiree health insurance, however, can retire from their full-time jobs and move to a different part-time or self-employment job while maintaining health insurance through their former employers. Research has shown that individuals with retiree health insurance are indeed much more likely to make a gradual transition from work to retirement than are individuals without retiree health insurance. Interestingly, many older workers, when asked, express a desire to make a gradual transition from work to retirement. Thus, health insurance that is portable across the transition from work to retirement appears to be an institution that enables individuals to retire both when and how they desire (Rust and Phelan 1997).

Understanding how health insurance affects retirement incentives is a particularly important policy issue because the retirement decisions of older individuals could be affected quite substantially in the upcoming years by changes in the institutions that provide health insurance to retirees—a resizing of the pieces in the patchwork quilt, if you will. The first important change is a dramatic decline in the number of employers that offer retiree health insurance. The fraction of employers offering retiree health insurance has fallen by almost half over the past 15 years, in large part because the escalation in medical care costs has made retiree health insurance an incredibly expensive benefit to provide. This erosion in the availability of retiree health insurance coverage will make retirement before the age of 65 much more difficult for many workers. Based on the evidence in the research that I have summarized so far, there will likely be an eventual increase in the average retirement age if the availability of retiree health insurance were the only factor affecting retirement that continued to change. While there has been no research to date explicitly focused on the decline in the availability of retiree health insurance and its effect on retirement, it is interesting to note that the decades-long trend in the declining average retirement age of men ended in 1985, at about the same time that employers began to drop their retiree health insurance plans.

A second potential major change in the health insurance landscape for older workers is the prospect of Medicare reform. There is almost universal consensus in both academic and policy circles that, for any number of reasons, Medicare needs to be reformed. Unfortunately, disagreement on exactly how it should be reformed has resulted in legislative paralysis. There have, however, been numerous proposals to reform Medicare, each of which would affect the labor force participation decisions of older workers in different ways. For example, the Breaux-Thomas proposal that came out of the recently disbanded Medicare reform commission would have raised the Medicare eligibility age to conform with the scheduled increase in the Social Security normal retirement age from 65 to 67. This change would delay retirement for those individuals without access to retiree health insurance, a group which, as just noted, is increasing in size as employers opt out of the retiree health insurance business. In addition, increasing the age of

Medicare eligibility would increase the cost to employers of providing retiree health insurance, and would likely provide even greater incentives for employers to relinquish their retiree health insurance plans. Thus, increasing the age of Medicare eligibility is likely to lead to increases in the average retirement age, both directly through the effect on retirement incentives of individuals without retiree health insurance, and indirectly through the incentive it creates for employers to abandon their retiree health insurance plans.

President Clinton presented a different Medicare reform proposal that would allow all individuals between the ages of 62 and 64 to buy into the Medicare program. By making Medicare available earlier, even though at a nonsubsidized price, this type of reform would actually motivate retirement at younger ages, reinforcing the decades-long trend toward earlier retirement.

Whether the current average retirement age is too high, too low, or just right is a normative question that perhaps warrants an entire chapter of its own. The point is that the health insurance landscape for older workers is currently changing in a very important way as employers give up their retiree health insurance plans, and it is likely to change even further as Congress will eventually make reforms to the Medicare program. These changes will certainly affect not only the retirement decisions of older workers, but also the savings and consumption decisions of younger workers as they make future plans for retirement. The overall economic implications of these changes could be tremendous.

HEALTH INSURANCE AND LABOR
FORCE PARTICIPATION

While much of the research on how health insurance affects labor force participation has been directed at the issue of retirement, older individuals are not the only ones whose employment decisions are affected by health insurance. Because the vast majority of prime-aged men work regardless of whether they receive employer-provided health insurance, it is women whose labor force participation decisions are most likely to be influenced by the availability of health insurance. One specific group of women for whom health insurance is likely to be particularly important are unskilled, less-educated, single mothers. As parents, they are apt to have a higher demand for health insurance coverage than single women without children. But, as single parents, they do not have access to health insurance coverage through their spouses. And, as unskilled single parents, they are qualified primarily for low-wage jobs—jobs that are much less likely to come with health insurance. One source of health insurance coverage that is potentially available to these women is Medicaid. However, until recently, welfare participation was a virtual precondition for the receipt of Medicaid benefits: employment that generated income sufficient to disqualify an individual from receiving further welfare benefits also disqualified an individual from further receipt of Medicaid. Thus, many less-skilled female workers have faced a choice between not working or working part time and receiving Medicaid, or working full time and losing both welfare benefits and Medicaid coverage.

An interesting change in the Medicaid eligibility rules in the late 1980s and early 1990s has made it possible to disentangle the impact of Medicaid eligibility on labor force participation from that of general welfare eligibility. A series of federal and state legislative initiatives have allowed women to maintain their Medicaid coverage for a pre-specified period of time after leaving welfare and extended indefinitely Medicaid coverage to many groups of low-income children. These changes effectively make Medicaid portable across the transition from welfare to work for a finite period for welfare recipients themselves, and for a much longer period for their children. Empirical research suggests that this type of Medicaid portability increases both the labor force participation and the hours worked of low-income single mothers (Yelowitz 1995). The former link between Medicaid and welfare participation was, in fact, a deterrent in motivating welfare recipients to find full-time work.

Married women are another group whose labor force participation is likely to be influenced by the availability of health insurance coverage. As already noted, prime-aged men are likely to work regardless of the availability of health insurance. In contrast, married women's labor supply has historically tended to be much more sensitive to the financial incentives associated with work, one of which is health insurance. Because most companies that offer health insurance make it available to both employees and their spouses, many married women receive

health insurance coverage through their husbands. Whether or not a married woman has health insurance through her spouse turns out to be a very important factor in whether and how much she works. Married women with health insurance through their husbands are substantially less likely to work than are women without health insurance from their spouses. And those who do work are much more likely to be employed in part-time rather than full-time jobs—jobs that typically do not provide health insurance (Buchmueller and Valetta 1999; Olson 1998). Thus, for married women, the lack of health insurance from a spouse's employment seems to have a strong influence in motivating married women to find jobs with health insurance themselves.

A recent study of married women's labor supply in Spain uncovered another interesting link between health insurance finance and female labor supply. In Spain, health care is provided by the government and financed out of a mandatory payroll tax paid partially by the firm and partially by the employee. Payment of the payroll tax entitles workers, their spouses, and dependent children to health care, as well as to a pension and sick leave. Among men, compliance with the payroll tax is universal. Among married women, however, over one-quarter of those who are employed work in the "underground" economy where "required" taxes are not paid (de la Rica and Lemieux 1994).

There are many other less-studied avenues through which health insurance is likely to affect labor supply. There is some evidence that the availability of health insurance during times of unemployment affects both the likelihood of and the duration of an unemployment spell (Gruber and Madrian 1997). The link between Medicare coverage and the receipt of Social Security Disability Insurance for disabled individuals under the age of 65 could act as a deterrent for work among the disabled, or at least work that would be sufficient to disqualify them from further disability benefits and the Medicare coverage that accompanies these benefits. University-provided health insurance to students operates in a similar way; individuals can participate in student health plans if they maintain their student status, which typically involves registering for a certain number of credit hours and maintaining satisfactory grades. Employment, or at least full-time employment, may jeopardize an individual's ability to maintain status as a student. Thus, some students who value their health insurance may be deterred from entering the labor market.

HEALTH INSURANCE AND JOB TURNOVER

Health insurance also affects the types of jobs in which individuals are employed. I have already noted that health insurance affects not only labor force participation, but also the choice of full- or part-time work for older individuals contemplating retirement, for married women, and for single women on welfare. Beyond the full- or part-time dimension of job choice, health insurance also influences the choice between various full-time jobs for those who want to work full-time—not only the initial choice of where to work, but also subsequent decisions about whether or not to change jobs. Economists are interested in the issue of job turnover because it is the process by which workers are reallocated away from jobs where they are less productive and into jobs where they are more productive. Impediments to productivity-enhancing job turnover are thus a barrier to economic growth. To make this point in a rather extreme way, imagine how different your life and the whole economy would be if your first employer were also your only employer; that is, if you could never change jobs.

Why does health insurance influence job turnover? One obvious reason is that not all employers offer health insurance. Individuals who have employer-provided health insurance and place a high value on it will be reluctant to switch to a company that doesn't provide health insurance. On the flip side, individuals who don't have employer-provided health insurance and who place a high value on it will be trying to switch to companies that do provide health insurance. An interesting piece of evidence on this front comes from the behavior of married men who are working in jobs without health insurance. Married men without health insurance but who have pregnant wives are twice as likely to change jobs as married men without health insurance whose wives are not pregnant (Madrian 1994b). The impending birth of a child clearly increases the value of health insurance, and these men respond by changing jobs, presumably in an attempt to find work with health insurance.

A second reason that health insurance affects the job turnover decisions of individuals is that not all employer-provided health insurance plans are equal, at least not for an employee who contemplates changing jobs. In addition to variation among employers in the generosity of the health insurance package in terms of co-payments, deductibles, and what is covered, there are two more subtle issues to consider. The first is that many employers exclude preexisting conditions for a certain period of time. So, even though a new employer and one's current employer may appear to provide identical coverage, the coverage of the new employer may in fact be vastly inferior for families with medical problems if these problems are not covered under the terms of a preexisting conditions exclusion restriction. The second issue is that in the era of managed care, employees do not generally have free choice among medical providers. Thus, an employment change that is accompanied by a health insurance change is also likely to necessitate a medical provider change. Individuals who value relationships with their current doctors may thus be averse to changing health insurance plans even if preexisting conditions are not an issue.

My own research on the relationship between health insurance and job turnover and that of others confirms that health insurance is an important factor in the decision to change jobs. One interesting finding is that among individuals who have employer-provided health insurance, those who also have coverage through the employment of a spouse are much more likely to change jobs than those who do not (Madrian 1994b; Buchmueller and Valetta 1996). In essence, health insurance coverage through a spouse's employment is portable across the transition from one job to another and is one way to skirt the preexisting conditions exclusions that may be in place at a new employer. Another interesting finding is that COBRA, in addition to motivating retirement among older workers, also motivates job turnover among younger workers (Gruber and Madrian 1994). COBRA makes the health insurance from one's former employer portable across jobs, at least for a limited time, but apparently long enough for many to skirt preexisting conditions exclusions.

One particular type of job transition, the movement to self-employment, is also likely to be influenced by the availability of health insurance. The self-employed owners of firms do not generally get the same tax advantages from purchasing health insurance as do employees. Moreover, because most of the self-employed tend to be sole proprietors or have very small firms, they are not able to take advantage of the economies of scale in health insurance provision available to large firms, or the benefits that large firms have in reducing the negative impact of adverse selection on the costs of insuring their employees. Thus, the health insurance costs of becoming self-employed may be nontrivial. Some research suggests that health insurance is indeed a factor in the decision about whether or not to become self-employed, and that individuals for whom the loss of health insurance is less costly (for example, those with health insurance through a spouse) are more likely to switch from employment to self-employment (Madrian and Lefgren 1998).

The likelihood of a future layoff—involuntary job turnover—may also affect the job choice decisions of individuals who place a high value on health insurance. Several years ago I had an MBA student who had been recently diagnosed with multiple sclerosis, a condition that would almost surely be classified as a preexisting condition. Upon hearing about my research interests, he told me that although he really wanted to work for a consulting firm and had indeed received offers to do so, he had decided to accept a job with a large manufacturing company with essentially a policy of lifetime employment. He reasoned that consulting companies have a reputation for promoting only a very small fraction of their hires to partner; the rest either leave or are dismissed within the first few years. Given his medical situation, he felt that it would be imprudent to accept a job in which there would be uncertainty regarding his future health insurance coverage as a result of the inherent uncertainty in the long-term job prospects at a consulting firm.

HEALTH INSURANCE AND THE EMPLOYMENT DECISIONS OF FIRMS

It is also interesting to consider the relationship between health insurance and job turnover from the employer's perspective. For an employer who offers health insurance coverage, sick employees (or healthy employees with sick dependents) are costly in two ways: they may be less productive and they are likely to generate higher insurance claims. Because of their medical expenditures, these employees may be relatively more attractive targets for layoffs. The link between health insurance and employment may thus have an adverse effect on families with medical problems if these problems lead to claims-based layoffs. Although I have seen no formal analysis of the prevalence of this type of layoff behavior, there is certainly anecdotal evidence that it does occur.

In addition to its effect on the employment and job choice decisions of individuals, health insurance may also influence the labor demand decisions of employers. There are two features of health insurance provision that are particularly salient in this regard. The first is that health insurance is a fixed cost of employment. Expected employer expenditures on health insurance do not increase when the weekly hours worked by their employees increase, and they do not increase when compensation increases; they only increase when more employees are hired. This feature of health insurance, its fixed-cost nature, gives firms an incentive to economize on the costs of providing health insurance in two ways: by hiring fewer employees but at longer weekly hours, which is one way to maintain production while reducing the overall costs of providing health insurance, and by hiring fewer but more productive employees—employees who can produce more than the average employee would. Some of my own research done in conjunction with David Cutler provides partial evidence that firms have substituted longer weekly hours for fewer workers as health insurance costs have increased over recent years. Moreover, the effects are nontrivial. The increase in weekly hours associated with the increase in health insurance costs between 1980 and 1993 resulted in a change in average weekly hours among those with health insurance equivalent to roughly half the change in labor input that is observed in a typical recession (Cutler and Madrian 1999).

Anecdotally, there have been several strikes in recent years against companies such as General Motors over the issue of perceived excess overtime. Companies have scheduled their workers for overtime on a regular basis, sometimes as many as 20 hours per week, in order to avoid the health insurance and other fixed costs of employment associated with hiring new workers. The workers, preferring shorter hours to an overtime premium, have gone on strike in an effort to pressure the companies into hiring more workers.

The second feature of health insurance that is salient to the labor demand decision is the distinction between full- and part-time workers in the tax treatment of employer expenditures on health insurance. As already noted briefly, employer expenditures on health insurance are usually not subject to taxation; however, there is one caveat: employers must satisfy a set of IRS nondiscrimination rules which stipulate that if a firm is to provide health insurance, it must make it widely available to nearly all employees. In essence, employers cannot selectively decide that they will provide health insurance to some employees and not to others, either because of favoritism or as a cost-saving measure. However, certain groups of employees, namely part-time, temporary, and seasonal workers, are exempt from the requirements of the nondiscrimination rules. Thus, employers can deny health insurance coverage to part-time, temporary, and seasonal workers while still obtaining favorable tax treatment for their health insurance expenditures on full-time permanent employees. As health insurance becomes more expensive to provide, the nondiscrimination rules give employers an incentive to hire part-time and temporary workers in lieu of full-time workers as a way to economize on insurance expenditures. While there are many reasons behind the phenomenal growth in the temporary help industry over the past two decades, the increasing cost of providing health insurance is surely one of them.

More concrete evidence that employers substitute part-timers for full-timers in the face of higher health insurance costs comes from the state of Hawaii. In 1974, Hawaii mandated employer provision of health insurance to full-time but not part-time workers. Those industries most affected by the mandate, namely industries in which relatively few full-time workers were covered by health insurance initially, saw a large increase in the fraction of workers employed in part-time jobs following the mandate. Essentially, employers who were suddenly faced with large health insurance bills as a result of the mandate decided to substitute part-time workers for full-time workers as a way to skirt requirement of the new law. In contrast, industries in which almost all full-time employees were already receiving health insurance saw little shift in the fraction of full- versus part-time workers (Thurston 1997).

For firms, then, health insurance affects both the size and composition of the workforce that is employed. As health insurance becomes more costly to provide, employers have an incentive to reduce their health insurance costs by substituting overtime for employment, skilled labor for unskilled labor, and part-time and temporary workers for regular full-time employees.

CONCLUSION

There is an important relationship between labor market outcomes and the institutions and rules governing health insurance provision in the United States. Health insurance is an important factor in almost every labor market decision made by individuals: whether to work, where to work, how many hours to work, and so on. It is also an important factor in the human resource decisions made by employers: how many workers to hire, whom to hire, how to structure the terms and conditions of employment.

But, given that there are many factors that affect the labor market decisions of individuals and firms, why the special concern with health insurance? Because our health care system continues to evolve in ways that influence important labor market outcomes. Significant changes in the health insurance institutions of the United States have taken place over the past 15 years. These include

- the implementation of COBRA, which provides limited health insurance portability to workers covered by employer-provided health insurance,
- passage of HIPAA, which attempts to further increase the amount of health insurance portability in the economy,
- the extension of Medicaid benefits to pregnant women and low-income children regardless of parental participation in either state welfare programs or the labor market,
- the shift away from fee-for-service medicine and toward managed care,
- the tax deductibility of health insurance expenditures of the self-employed,
- small business health insurance pools,
- a dramatic decline in employer provision of retiree health insurance, and

- a proliferation in state-mandated health insurance benefits.

And even more substantive changes continue to be proposed, such as

- changes in the Medicare eligibility age,
- changes in or elimination of the tax-deductibility of health insurance and other employee benefits,
- mandatory community rating of health premiums insurance in the nongroup market,
- further expansions in the availability of publicly provided health insurance, and, of course,
- broad-based national health care reform, an issue that is not widely discussed at the moment but, if history is our guide, will surely resurface at some point in the future.

The merits of these various proposals depend on a variety of things. While most discussion tends to focus on access to health care services and the government budget, it is also important to consider the impact of these proposals on the labor market. Do they promote or impede labor market efficiency? Do they distort the labor supply choices that individuals otherwise would have made? Do they change the hiring decisions of firms?

These issues are perhaps most important not in the United States, but in the developing countries of the world that are currently struggling to design and implement their own health care and health insurance institutions. An important lesson to be learned from the experience of the United States is that while employer provision of health insurance is a convenient way to finance insurance benefits without involving the government budget directly, not everyone is tied to the labor market. Reliance on and encouragement of employer provision of health insurance will invariably result in government programs to fill in the gaps and cover the otherwise uninsured. But it is the interplay between these various institutions, some tied directly to the labor market and others not, that results in distortions of the labor market decisions of individuals and firms.

Is there a way to eliminate the labor market distortions associated with health insurance provision in the United States? Yes and no; one way would be to have nationalized health insurance that covered everyone regardless of employment status. Such an institution would provide no incentives to be employed or not employed, at least not on the basis of health insurance. However, such an institution would invariably involve distortions along other margins. For example, the tax revenue needed to finance nationalized health insurance would invariably create distortions in the markets that are taxed, quite possibly the labor market if financed through an income or payroll tax. This would, in essence, involve trading one set of labor market distortions for another. It's a gloomy picture, isn't it?

The bottom line, then, is that any system of health insurance provision is likely to involve labor market distortions, either directly through the institutions themselves, or indirectly through the way they are financed. This is not necessarily bad—after all, many of the good things that are provided by the government involve trading one kind of market distortion for another: public education, roads and other forms of infrastructure, and national defense. By understanding the distortions, i.e., where they come from and how big they are, we can begin to make informed decisions about which types of reform will have the greatest beneficial impact on both health and economic efficiency.

References

Blau, David M., and Donna B. Gilleskie. 1997. "Retiree Health Insurance and the Labor Force Behavior of Older Men in the 1990s." Working paper no. 5948, National Bureau of Economic Research, Cambridge, Massachusetts.

Buchmueller, Thomas C., and Robert G. Valletta. 1996. "The Effect of Employer-Provider Health Insurance on Worker Mobility." *Industrial and Labor Relations Review* 49(3): 439–455.

_____. 1999. "The Effect of Health Insurance on Married Female Labor Supply." *Journal of Human Resources* 34(1): 42–70.

Cutler, David M., and Brigitte C. Madrian. 1999. "Labor Market Responses to Rising Health Insurance Costs: Evidence on Hours worked." *Rand Journal of Economics* 29(3): 509–530.

de la Rica, Sara, and Thomas Lemieux. 1994. "Does Public Health Insurance Reduce Labor Market Flexibility or Encourage the Underground Economy? Evidence from Spain and the United States." In *Social Protection*

Versus Economic Flexibility: Is There a Trade-Off?, Rebecca M. Blank, ed. Chicago, Illinois: University of Chicago Press, pp. 265–299.

Employee Benefit Research Institute. 1993. *Public Attitudes on Benefit Trade Offs.* Washington, D.C.: Employee Benefit Research Institute.

Gruber, Jonathan, and Brigitte C. Madrian. 1994. "Health Insurance and Job Mobility: The Effects of Public Policy on Job Lock." *Industrial and Labor Relations Review* 48(1): 86–102.

_____. 1995. "Health Insurance Availability and the Retirement Decision." *American Economic Review* 85(4): 938–948.

_____. 1997. "Employment Separation and Health Insurance Coverage." *Journal of Public Economics* 66(3): 349–382.

Gustman, Alan L., and Thomas L. Steinmeier. 1994. "Employer-Provided Health Insurance and Retirement Behavior." *Industrial and Labor Relations Review* 48(1): 124–140.

Karoly, Lynn, and Jeannette A. Rogowski. 1994. "The Effect of Access to Post Retirement Health Insurance on the Decision to Retire Early." *Industrial and Labor Relations Review* 48(1): 103–123.

Madrian, Brigitte C. 1994a. "The Effect of Health Insurance on Retirement." *Brookings Papers on Economic Activity* (1): 181–232.

_____. 1994b. "Employment-Based Health Insurance and Job Mobility: Is There Evidence of Job Lock?" *Quarterly Journal of Economics* 109(1): 27–54.

Madrian, Brigitte C., and Nancy D. Beaulieu. 1998. "Does Medicare Eligibility Affect Retirement?" In *Inquiries in the Economics of Aging,* David A. Wise, ed. Chicago, Illinois: University of Chicago Press, pp. 109–131.

Madrian, Brigitte C., and Lars J. Lefgren. 1998. "The Effect of Health Insurance on Transitions to Self Employment." Unpublished paper, University of Chicago, Chicago, Illinois.

Olson, Craig A. 1998. "A Comparison of Parametric and Semiparametric Estimates of the Effect of Spousal Health Insurance Coverage on Weekly Hours Worked by Wives." *Journal of Applied Econometrics* 13(5): 543–565.

Rogowski, Jeannette A., and Lynn Karoly. 2000. "Health Insurance and Retirement Behavior: Evidence from the Health and Retirement Survey." *Journal of Health Economics* 19(4): 529–539.

Rust, John, and Christopher Phelan. 1997. "How Social Security and Medicare Affect Retirement Behavior in a World of Incomplete Markets." *Econometrica* 65(4): 781–831.

Thurston, Norman K. 1997. "Labor Market Effects of Hawaii's Mandatory Employer-Provided Health Insurance." *Industrial and Labor Relations Review* 51(1): 117–135.

Yelowitz, Aaron S.   1995.   "The Medical Notch, Labor Supply and Welfare Participation: Evidence from Eligibility Expansions." *Quarterly Journal of Economics* 110(4): 909–940.

5

Health Care Consumer Choice
The Role of Information

Catherine G. McLaughlin
University of Michigan

Choice is a highly prized commodity in the United States. The freedom to choose is fiercely protected. Recently health care consumers have felt as though their freedom to choose has been threatened: when they seek care, from whom, and how often; the site of treatment, whether inpatient or outpatient; whether they can spend a third day in the hospital after a normal delivery; whether they can purchase generic rather than brand-name drugs. Rightly or wrongly, they blame a lot of this loss of freedom on the growth of managed care. We are witnessing a plethora of articles and stories in the mainstream press, on television, even in movies like *As Good As It Gets*, as well as testimony at federal and state legislative committee hearings debating Patient Bill of Rights legislation.[1]

What most people may not realize is that before a consumer, a patient, ever reaches an individual health care provider's office to discuss a particular diagnosis and treatment, a myriad of decisions have been made—decisions that influence the selection of the provider, the treatment, and how much the treatment will cost the patient. The typical health care consumer faces a road map of options, and the consequences of taking one option instead of the other are always attached to those choices. In many cases, when consumers make one choice, they are getting on a one-way road with that choice leading to future constraints.

As illustrated in Figure 1, for some adults the first choice that may in part be conditioned on an individual's desire for health insurance coverage is whether to enter the labor market. The role played by Medicaid in the welfare-to-work decision is frequently discussed. Less attention is paid to the effect of health insurance coverage on other

Figure 1 Labor Market and Health Insurance Choices

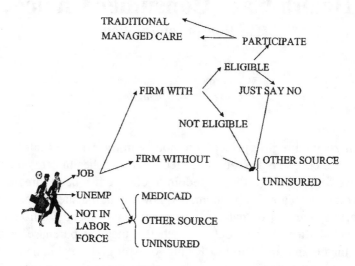

populations, but the desire for affordable health insurance may also influence the labor market decisions of those not eligible for Medicaid, such as spouses of working adults without employment-based insurance.

Adults who do not seek employment or who are unsuccessful in finding a job end up either covered by Medicaid, obtaining insurance through another source (e.g., a spouse's plan or a plan obtained in the nongroup market), or uninsured.

VARIATION IN FIRM OFFER RATES

The decision of what kind of firm in which to seek employment is also influenced by the demand for health insurance. Health insurance options vary by firm. While health insurance is but one factor in firm choice, it's not difficult to believe that young, single males may deliberately choose to supply their labor to a small, high-tech firm that offers no health insurance in exchange for higher wages. It is also understandable that a young male who has similar skills but who has a wife and two small children may choose instead to supply his labor to a large corporation, earning a lower salary but receiving a rich family health insurance package at a large group rate.

Approximately 25 percent of working adults are employed by firms that do not offer health insurance (McLaughlin 1999a). Small firms, those with 25 or fewer employees, are disproportionately represented in this group. While 90 percent of firms with 100 or more employees offer some kind of group health insurance package to their workers, less than half of those with fewer than 10 employees do so. These differences in offer rates have been fairly constant over time and stem from a variety of labor and insurance market differences (Brown, Hamilton, and Medoff 1990; McLaughlin and Zellers 1992).

Affordability

A survey of approximately 2,000 small businesses in seven cities revealed that the reasons for not offering a group health insurance policy to their employees could be grouped into three different categories summarized as affordability, employee attitudes, and availability (McLaughlin and Zellers 1994). The number-one reason given in this and other surveys is dollars; virtually all small business owners say that high and rising health insurance premiums are the primary reason for not offering health insurance. The lack of affordable health insurance products is a central problem for small businesses and their employees. Many small businesses operate on low profit margins and face premiums 10–40 percent higher than those paid by large firms (GAO 1992). The convergence of low profit margins, low wages, and high premiums means than neither employers nor employees in small businesses can easily trade revenue or wages for health insurance.

Attitudes

The failure of many small businesses to purchase health insurance has as much to do with attitudes and perceptions as with affordability. The majority of owners who did not offer insurance (61 percent) said that they had no interest in offering any (McLaughlin and Zellers 1994). To some degree, this attitude reflects the nature of the business.

For example, one shrimper in Tampa said, "I go to the dock every morning and say 'You, you, and you, jump on board.' What am I supposed to do? Get them to sign a Blue Cross and Blue Shield contract for the day?"[2] In addition, many small businesses have very loosely defined or temporal employment contracts with their workers (e.g., taxi cab drivers, construction workers).

The driving force behind this lack of interest, however, was the belief that their workers did not want coverage, that they preferred higher wages to health insurance. In contrast to what many workers apparently believe, the employer does not pay for health insurance. Regardless of who writes the premium check, the workers and consumers pay for insurance through lower wage growth and higher prices (Pauly 1997); the owners surveyed felt as though their workers were not willing to make the trade. Many of these employees can piggyback on the (usually better value) health plans of spouses' employers, which appears to be a key reason why many companies do not provide coverage for their employees. Because employees of these other firms rarely pay the full marginal cost of having family coverage (either directly through higher out-of-pocket premiums or indirectly through lower wage growth), employees who have this safety net for coverage often prefer to be compensated in higher wages rather than in benefits. In firms where employers responded that their employees' ability to get insurance elsewhere was a very important reason for not offering insurance, 73 percent of the employees did obtain health insurance from another source (McLaughlin and Zellers 1994).

Availability

There was another reason for lack of coverage, however. Some of these owners would have been interested in providing group coverage but expressed difficulty obtaining insurance because of insurance underwriting procedures. For one out of five small businesses without insurance, the lack of insurance can be attributed to redlining and preexisting condition exclusions (redlining is the exclusion of specific types of businesses from eligibility for coverage). Insurers may designate a business unacceptable if they consider employees of these businesses to be at a higher risk for illness or injury because of occupation, age, lifestyles, etc.

Virtually all insurers of small businesses engage in a practice known as redlining, drawing a red line across the list of risks, making all industries with risks above that amount ineligible for insurance (Zellers et al. 1992). McLaughlin and Zellers also surveyed insurance companies and independent agents in the same seven cities participating in the employer survey, as well as the 10 national companies with the largest book of business in the small group market. They asked for examples of industries that are routinely redlined and received underwriting brochures from 20 different companies.

Eighty-five percent of insurance agents and 48 percent of insurance company representatives said they redline specific types of businesses. Seven percent of all small business employees whose companies do not offer insurance are excluded because of redlining practices. As shown in Figure 2, redlined industries are not just those industries such as asbestos removal firms and mining and logging companies that have hazardous working conditions. Major employers such as restaurants, bars, hair salons, physician offices, and law offices are also commonly redlined. About 15 percent of small firms are in industries that are routinely redlined (Zellers et al. 1992).

Figure 2 Types of Redlined Businesses

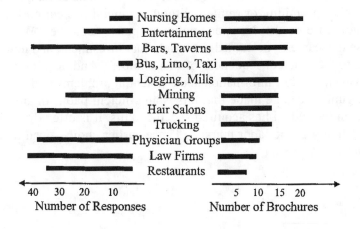

SOURCE: McLaughlin and Zellers (1994).

Employees in redlined industries are considered "undesirable" not only because of working conditions but because of the age, other demographic characteristics, or lifestyles of employees. Redlined industries typically employ older workers (over age 55) and/or have high employee turnover, seasonal workforces, or workforces paid by commission or on the basis of other contractual terms. The hair salon industry is particularly illustrative of the problem faced by many of the employees of these businesses. As one insurer stated, these employees are seen by insurers as representing a "triple threat: lots of turnover, young women who get pregnant, and gays with the threat of AIDS." Physicians are seen as "heavy utilizers, hypochondriacs," and lawyers as "too litigious, they dispute every claim denied." [3]

While some of these individuals have the financial resources necessary to purchase insurance in the individual market or can obtain group insurance through professional organizations, this is not the case for some workers, such as hair stylists or professional musicians in local symphonies. These individuals decided, most likely in high school, to acquire the human capital necessary to become a professional in this field, not knowing that down the road, when they were no longer "young invincibles" but 30-year-old pregnant women or 40-year-olds with carpal tunnel syndrome or hypertension, they would have problems getting coverage because of their profession. At this point, they either have to change careers, learning new skills marketable to industries that are not redlined, seek individual coverage with a very high premium, or remain without financial protection for any medical care needs. Now, one policy response could be, "Well, you chose this career; you earned a return to that investment, and now you have to face the consequences of that choice." And, as long as that individual had full information about potential problems in the future, an argument can be made that this is an efficient path. In any case, once an individual has acquired specific skills, it is often difficult to move freely in the labor market. Those earlier choices lead to constraints.

VARIATION IN INDIVIDUAL PARTICIPATION RATES

Eligibility

Seventy-five percent of workers are employed by firms that do offer insurance (McLaughlin 1999a). Not all workers are eligible, however; approximately 5 percent of workers are not eligible for their firm's plan.

The most common reasons for being ineligible have to do with the employment contract, particularly working part time (Table 1). Analysis of the 1993 Current Population Survey (CPS) data shows that while 80 percent of full-time workers are offered insurance, only 19 percent of those working fewer than 20 hours a week are. Even this difference is mitigated by the size of firm, with more part-time workers offered health insurance by larger firms. In firms with 100 or more workers, the percentage of at least half-time workers offered health insurance is virtually the same as that of full-time workers. A worker's salary also influences whether or not she or he will be offered health insurance. Higher-paid workers are much more likely to be offered health insurance. Forty-three percent of workers earning less than $7 per hour are offered health insurance by their employers, whereas 93 percent of those earning more than $15 per hour are offered coverage (Cooper and Steinberg-Schone 1997). Once again, this difference narrows as the firm size increases (Bucci and Grant 1995). Younger workers are also less likely to be offered health insurance—only 51 percent of those younger than 25 years old are offered coverage (Cooper and Steinberg-Schone 1997).

Table 1 Reasons for Being Ineligible

- 26% are still in probationary period
- 9% are contract or temporary workers
- 58% are part-time workers
- 2% have preexisting conditions

SOURCE: 1993 Current Population Survey data reported in Yakoboski et al. (1994).

For a small percentage of workers, medical underwriting practices, specifically preexisting condition exclusion clauses, result in ineligibility. Preexisting condition exclusion clauses deny coverage to individuals for conditions for which they have received medical care in the past. With very small groups (fewer than 10 employees), it is not uncommon for an insurer to deny coverage to the entire business if one or more employees has a potentially high-cost preexisting condition.

Again, these barriers are more common in small businesses, not because workers are more likely to have preexisting conditions, but because insurance companies rarely check for these conditions, much less act on them, in large firms. Based on their survey, McLaughlin and Zellers estimated that 15–20 percent of the employees in small firms were ineligible for coverage, not just for the first six months of employment or just for the condition, but for any insurance policy.

Exclusions for preexisting conditions may be a primary reason for "job lock." (Cooper and Monheit 1993). These exclusions discourage workers from switching jobs because they or a family member may not be covered for a health problem under a new insurance plan or may lose coverage altogether. Some of these conditions are chronic conditions and can therefore affect career choices.

McLaughlin and Zellers (1994) found that the most frequently excluded conditions were heart disease, cancer, diabetes, and AIDS (Figure 3). Heart disease was the medical condition that was more commonly excluded for coverage by insurance companies. Fifty-three of the 83 insurance company representatives and agents who were asked about their preexisting condition exclusion policies said they excluded coverage of heart disease for individuals who have already been diagnosed and treated for this condition. Other excluded conditions include mental or nervous conditions, degenerative nerve disorders such as muscular dystrophy and multiple sclerosis, kidney anomalies, and stroke. In some cases, insurers were unwilling to provide coverage for anyone in the firm if one worker had one of these conditions. Interestingly, insurers cited preexisting conditions or "health problems" as the main reason small businesses have difficulty obtaining health coverage.

Figure 3 Medical Conditions Frequently Excluded

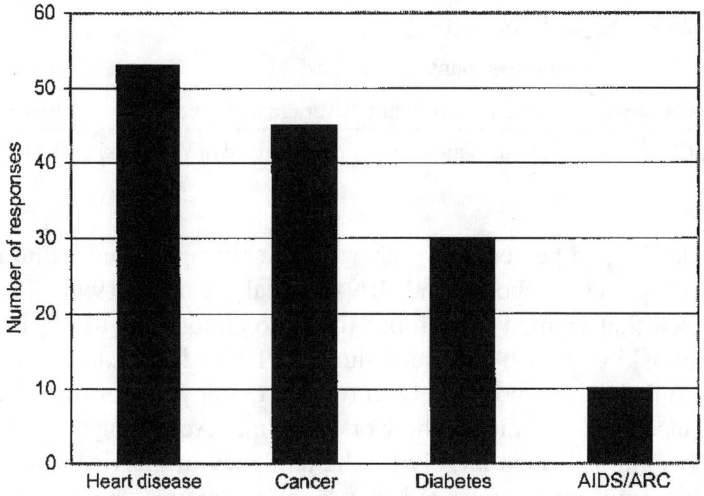

SOURCE: McLaughlin and Zellers (1994).

Employee Choice

Some workers who are eligible for coverage choose to "just say no." A recent study comparing household surveys from 1989 and 1996 reveals that a greater number of workers, particularly low-wage workers, are declining to take employer-sponsored insurance (Cooper and Steinberg-Schone 1997). The turn-down rate is higher among low-wage workers. A reasonable interpretation of these data is that these workers are not willing to pay the out-of-pocket premiums and hope to trade at least some wage growth for health insurance. In the 1996 national survey, 80 percent of workers who were offered a plan chose to participate. In contrast, only 63 percent of workers earning less than $7 per hour chose to participate. Less than 50 percent of those working part time chose to participate, in addition to 70 percent of those under age 25 and 74 percent of those working in firms with fewer than 25 employees (Cooper and Steinberg-Schone 1997).

In addition, as noted in Table 2, some workers choose not to participate because they have insurance through another source. Of those

Table 2 Reasons for Choosing not to Participate

- 75% have other source of coverage
- 23% say plan is too costly
- 2% say plan has too many limitations
- 6% say they don't need or want coverage

SOURCE: 1993 Current Population Survey data reported in Yakoboski et al. (1994).

who decline, 75 percent have other group coverage, usually through a spouse's plan (Yakoboski et al. 1994). Analysis of the 1993 CPS data revealed that women were more likely to choose not to participate (Yakoboski et al. 1994). Buchmueller (1996) found that men who work full time are more likely to receive employer-sponsored health insurance than are women who work full time. According to his analysis, this gap is driven largely by the tendency of married women to decline employer-sponsored insurance in favor of being covered through their husband's employer's insurance policy.

The availability of another source of insurance enables many workers to choose employment in the small business community, to say no to costly or undesirable plans, to elect to stay home and engage in child-rearing, or to obtain further training and education. It is also, however, the source of inequities. Employers rarely charge employees, either directly or indirectly, the full marginal cost of choosing a family plan rather than a single plan. Therefore, single workers (or married workers with a spouse covered by employment-based insurance who elect single coverage) subsidize workers who choose family coverage at reduced prices. While society may decide that this subsidy is an efficient way to enable parents to stay home or spouses to remain in school, problems of horizontal inequity arise between similar workers of large firms and small firms.

Not all workers who decline coverage or work for a firm without coverage have insurance through another source; a significant number of them are uninsured. In fact, 85 percent of the uninsured are workers and their dependents (McLaughlin 1999a). The number of medically uninsured adults and children is steadily increasing and is the cause of many policy recommendations, at both the federal and state level.

While some people are uninsured because of underwriting conditions, most are not. Many workers are eligible for coverage yet decline; others work in firms that do not offer coverage. These two groups of workers are very similar in measured characteristics: young, lower wage, and single (Long and Marquis 1993; Cooper and Steinberg-Schone 1997).

In some cases, these uninsured workers feel that they do not need coverage. They are basing this decision on their known health status and past experience. Unfortunately, if one of these workers is in a car accident, or develops cancer or diabetes, we do not say, "Too bad, you made your choice and chose not to trade wages for health insurance. Now we choose not to provide care for you." In part, we recognize that there is poor information about future needs, about the probability of an exogenous shock to our health status, and we decide to provide care for them that is then subsidized by those who chose to make the trade.

Chernew et al. (1997) estimated the subsidy amount necessary to prompt voluntary participation in health insurance. They estimated that for a significant number of workers, the subsidy would have to be almost as large as the premium; therefore, the welfare loss of mandating that they trade wages for health insurance would be quite high. There is a high price to taking away people's choice.

CHOICE OF PLANS

Finally, we get to those workers who choose to participate; they remain the majority of working adults. Half of these workers have no choice in plan, and most of them are offered only a traditional fee-for-service plan. Half of those with choice are offered only one or more traditional plans; about one-third are offered only one or more managed care plans. For many workers, the choice of employer determines the choice of plan. Although the percentage of firms offering more than one health care plan is increasing, it is still the case that the majority of all firms offer only one plan (McLaughlin 1999a).

As shown in Table 3, just as being offered any plan varies by firm size, so does the availability of choice of plan types. The percentage of firms offering more than one plan increases with firm size—as low as

Table 3 Combinations of Plan Types Offered by Employers, by Firm Size

Combinations of plan types[a]	% of firms that offer		% of full-time workers offered	
	Firm <100 workers	Firm 100+ workers	Firm <100 workers	Firm 100+ workers
FFS only	74	44	62	32
HMO only	8	8	11	6
PPO only	12	18	14	15
FFS + HMO	3	17	7	22
FFS + PPO	1	2	1	2
HMO + PPO	2	9	3	14
FFS + HMO + PPO	<0.5	3	1	9

SOURCE: Bucci and Grant (1995); BLS data for 1992–1993.
[a] FFS = fee-for-service; HMO = health maintenance organization; PPO = preferred-provider organization.

10 percent of firms with fewer than 100 employees and rising to 90 percent of firms with 5,000 or more employees (McLaughlin 1999a). A 1996 KPMG survey found that only 9 percent of employees of firms with fewer than 10 employees were offered a choice of plans, whereas 54 percent of employees of firms with more than 200 employees were offered choice (Gabel, Ginsburg, and Hunt 1997).

Of those firms that offer a choice, the majority offer a choice between two plans (Bucci and Grant 1995). About one-fifth offer a choice between three plans, and a few offer more than three plans from which to choose. About one-half of all workers with choice are offered two plans, one-fifth are offered three plans, and the rest are offered four or more. Again, the tendency to offer multiple plans increases with firm size. A 1997 Mercer survey estimated that 56 percent of companies with 3,000 or more employees offer three or four plan types (Mercer's Fax Facts 1997).

It turns out that for many of us, the choice of health insurance is an important one. Once enrolled in a particular plan, consumers are constrained by the specifics of the plan. The decisions about when to seek care and which provider to use are influenced by the type and financial incentives of the plan. The choice of treatment is also constrained by plan specifics. A person who is a risk-taker and who would want every possible treatment known, whether experimental or well-established, if faced with a life-threatening disease, would want a different kind of plan than a person who is more conservative in treatment choice. An employer can use health insurance options to influence the kind of worker seeking employment in that firm. For example, offering a sub-sidized family coverage benefit may discourage single workers and encourage young workers with families. A firm whose work requires risk-taking may want to offer a high-deductible plan.

LIMITATIONS TO CHOICE

One of the basic principles of managed care is reduced choice, par-ticularly reduced choice of provider. In general, healthier individuals, those who anticipate needing very little interaction with the medical care sector, are going to be less sensitive to this reduced choice. The resulting enrollment of healthier workers, combined with a host of financial incentives and structural aspects, has led to lower premiums. These lower premiums, coupled with low co-pays, particularly for pharmaceuticals, have encouraged consumers to overcome their aver-sion to reduced choice and elect to enroll in managed care plans when given a choice.

Much of the unhappiness with the managed care market results from lack of information. When surveyed, most enrollees focus on the reduced premia and co-pays and express ignorance about limited choice (Mechanic et al. 1990). When they then get sick and become acutely aware of the limitations, they are unpleasantly surprised and angry (McLaughlin 1999b). Of course, the response can be, "Well, you chose lower costs over limited choice. Now you must live with the consequences." Again, this is assuming that they were fully informed about the consequences of their choice, that they were able to read and understand the fine print in their insurance contract. If workers receive more information, some may choose the traditional plan instead. For the one-third of workers who had no choice other than managed care, the only option is to seek employment in another firm.

In some important ways, the individual who chooses to self-insure faces the least constraints; he or she is free to choose any willing provider. Of course, lack of money greatly reduces this freedom for many. In fact, one could say that for most people, the major constraint to choice is money.

At this point, it is clear that these decisions at the endpoint work back through the other decisions. The perceived need for freedom of choice of provider and treatment may reflect knowledge of medical need, which in turn influences the desire to enter the workforce to begin with. The decision process is certainly not a nice, neat linear model of consumer choice. Rather, it is more like the highways around Los Angeles, looping under and over, with complex figure eights, and equally congested and frustrating to the analyst. Unfortunately, private and public policymakers considering policies that address issues of health insurance choice must look at all the various pieces, recognizing that a change in the relative prices or options faced at one dyad will affect other choices. Only when researchers provide better estimates of the likely size of these so-called unintended consequences will policymakers be able to develop policies that yield the desired effects.

Notes

1. See, for example, *Journal of Health Politics, Policy and Law* 24:5. Special Issue: The Managed Care Backlash, Mark A. Peterson (ed.), 1999.
2. From author interviews.
3. From author interviews.

References

Brown, C., J. Hamilton, and J. Medoff. 1990. *Employers Large and Small.* Cambridge, Massachusetts: Harvard University Press.

Bucci, Michael, and Robert Grant. 1995. "Employer-Sponsored Health Insurance: What's Offered, What's Chosen?" *Monthly Labor Review* October: 38–44.

Buchmueller, Thomas C. 1996. "Marital Status, Spousal Coverage, and the Gender Gap in Employer-Sponsored Health Insurance." *Inquiry* 33(4): 308–316.

Chernew, Michael E., Kevin Frick, and Catherine G. McLaughlin. 1997. "The Demand for Health Insurance by Low Income Workers: Can Reduced

Premiums Achieve Full Coverage?" *Health Services Research* 32(4): 453–470.

Cooper, Philip F., and Alan C. Monheit. 1993. "Does Employment-Related Health Insurance Inhibit Job Mobility?" *Inquiry* 30(Winter): 400–416.

Cooper, Philip F., and Barbara Steinberg-Schone. 1997. "More Offers, Fewer Takers for Employment-Based Health Insurance: 1987 and 1996." *Health Affairs* 16(6):142–149.

GAO. 1992. "Employer-Based Health Insurance: High Costs, Wide Variation Threaten System." U.S. General Accounting Office report, GAO/HRD-92-125, September.

Gabel, Jon R., Paul B. Ginsburg, and Kelly A. Hunt. 1997. "Small Employers and Their Health Benefits, 1988–1996: An Awkward Adolescence." *Health Affairs* 16(5):103–110.

Long, Stephen H., and M. Susan Marquis. 1993. "Gaps in Employer Coverage: Lack of Supply or Demand?" *Health Affairs* 12(Supplement): 282–293.

McLaughlin, Catherine G. 1999a. "Health Care Consumers: Choices and Constraints." *Medical Care Research and Review* 56(1): 24–59.

_____. 1999b. "The Who, What, and How of Managed Care." *The Journal of Health Politics, Policy and Law* 24(5): 1045–1049.

McLaughlin, Catherine G., and Wendy K. Zellers. 1992. "The Shortcoming of Voluntarism in the Small-Group Insurance Market." *Health Affairs* 11(2): 28–40.

_____. 1994. *Small Business and Health Reform.* Ann Arbor, Michigan: University of Michigan Press.

Mechanic, David, Therese Ettel, and Diane Davis. 1990. "Choosing among Health Insurance Options: A Study of New Employees." *Inquiry* 27: 14–23.

William H. Mercer, Inc. 1997. "Mercer's Fax Facts Surveys: HMOs." William H. Mercer, Inc., New York, April.

Pauly, M. 1997. *Health Benefits at Work: An Economic and Political Analysis of Employment-Based Health Insurance.* Ann Arbor, Michigan: University of Michigan Press.

Yakoboski, P., P. Fronstin, S. Snider, A. Reilly, D. Scheer, B. Custer, and S. Boyce. 1994. "Employment-Based Health Benefits: Analysis of the April 1993 Current Population Survey." *EBRI Issue Brief* (152): 1–50.

Zellers, W.K., C.G. McLaughlin, and K.D. Frick. 1992. "Health Insurance for Small Businesses: Only the Healthy Need Apply." *Health Affairs* 11(1): 174–180.

6

Positive Economics and Dismal Politics

The Role of Tax Policy in the Current Health Policy Debate

Robert B. Helms
American Enterprise Institute

Those who have participated in this series for several years must have learned by now that economists do not view the world as others do. And those who have participated so far this year must have learned that this is especially true of those economists who specialize in health economics. Given that most of my career has been spent in Washington, it is my observation that economists play a very small role in the national health policy debate. While there is a grain of truth in the well-worn jokes about economists not being able to reach a conclusion, the reality is that health policy debates have been dominated throughout the twentieth century by strong groups of providers who have a direct stake in the outcome of legislation. In the last few years these groups have been joined by other groups claiming to represent "consumers" or specific groups of patients. All of these participants in the health policy debate provide ample employment to a new army of pollsters and political analysts willing to tell the politicians and the public what kind of health policies they think we want. In the midst of all this noise, the hard-working academic or government health economist, trained to ask fundamental questions and seek answers based on factual information, and having earned a reputation for producing overly technical and dull reports, has a difficult time being heard. The result is a political environment that has a higher probability of producing legislation based on emotion and wishful thinking than on the economist's usual standard of economic efficiency.

Nowhere is this danger for bad policy more prevalent than in the current health policy debate. Politicians are striving to legislate improvements in medical quality without asking why our current market arrangements have put too little emphasis on quality and consumer satisfaction. They are beginning to seek ways to reduce the number of uninsured without considering the root causes of why most of the uninsured choose not to buy insurance. Legislators are expressing more concern about the future of Medicare without considering how to get both consumers and providers more involved in the choice of productive and cost-effective medical plans and procedures. It is still my opinion that economists have a positive role to play in guiding health policies toward more efficient arrangements. Despite our reputation for dull reports, health economics is anything but a dismal science.

The purpose of this chapter is to give my own interpretation of a rather large body of economic literature about how modern medical markets have developed. The emphasis will be on the role that tax policy has played in shaping the distinctive form of health care institutions and incentives that characterize our market today. This background will then be used to comment on various tax policy changes being considered to make health insurance more available to the presently uninsured.

THE POSTWAR HISTORY OF THE
DEVELOPMENT OF HEALTH INSURANCE[1]

World War II provides a convenient demarcation in the history of medicine and health insurance. Numerous advances in scientific knowledge had been made prior to the war, but these advances were not generally available to the vast majority of Americans. Prior to the war there was little that the average physician could do for the average patient to change the course of a disease. That changed dramatically in the two decades following the war, especially as a result of the development of penicillin during the war and more powerful antibiotics after the war. These new drugs gave physicians the power to fight infection and made possible many of the surgical operations that we now take for granted. New research on medical products and procedures, and the wide dispersion of this new knowledge to a growing number of health professionals, made the average person more willing to seek medical care than in the earlier part of the century. The increased availability of more effective medical care changed expectations about what physicians could do and increased the demand for medical services. As one indication of this change, Somers and Somers (1961) reported that annual hospital admissions per 1,000 population increased from 56.7 during the period 1923–1943 to 99.4 for the period 1957–1958.

Not only was the average citizen more willing to seek medical care, but they were increasingly able to afford it. The postwar period is known as one of rapid growth in population, employment, productivity, and personal income. In 1982 constant dollars, disposable personal income increased from $5,285 in 1945 to $8,944 in 1975, an average annual growth rate of 1.77 percent over this 30-year period (U.S. Bureau of the Census 1990, table 695).

The increase in the demand for medical care was accompanied by a supply response from every factor market in the medical sector. In his history of the U.S. hospital sector, William White (1982) reported that, "Between 1940 and 1965 the total number of general hospitals in the country increased by nearly 40 percent, while the number of beds increased by over 85 percent." During this same period, the number of physicians increased 74 percent, while the number of nurses increased 116 percent (U.S. Bureau of the Census 1975).

These structural changes in the health care sector also had a strong effect on the way health care was paid for. The postwar increase in medical productivity and the infusion of large numbers of personnel and capital resources meant that the cost of medical care increased, both absolutely and relative to average incomes. The average consumer had a stronger incentive to worry about the cost of medical care because they faced a higher probability of going into a hospital and utilizing the services of highly trained medical specialists. This change in the medical market created a desire on the part of consumers to protect themselves against the small probability that they would face a large medical expense. This increase in the demand for risk avoidance created the favorable conditions for the growth of the private health insurance industry following the war.

But, medical science and higher income were not the only forces attributing to the growth in the health insurance industry. In fact, tax policy contributed significantly to both the rate of growth of private health insurance and many attributes of its structure and performance.

Again, the role of tax policy in health markets had its origins in World War II.

Glied (1994) pointed out that the exclusion of health benefits provided by an employer "existed implicitly since the inception of the federal income tax in 1913." But with almost no demand for health insurance prior to the war, this provision had little effect until labor market conditions changed during the war. In an effort to control the cost of war production, the federal government established wage and price controls during the war. With the expanding demand for labor, the wage controls created a classic case of excess demand and gave employers strong incentives to increase fringe benefits and other non-wage components of employment. These inducements primarily took the form of the provision of pensions and health insurance, a practice that received official sanction by the War Labor Board in 1943. Field and Shapiro (1993) stated that, "In a war economy with labor shortages, employer contributions for employee health benefits became a means of maneuvering around wage controls. By the end of the war, health coverage had tripled." After some vacillation by the IRS following the war, the Congress made the exclusion of employer-based health insurance from taxable income a permanent feature of tax law in 1954.[2]

While this special tax treatment for employer-based health insurance was established for other reasons, it ended up having a profound effect on the development of health insurance and, in turn, on the development of the entire medical sector. While other forms of insurance were growing in the postwar period in response to the increase in consumer incomes and the desire to protect against financial losses, tax policy caused the health insurance industry to grow primarily by the growth in group policies rather than individual insurance. As illustrated in Figure 1, group health insurance grew at a much faster rate than individual insurance in the postwar period covering 158 million persons relative to 43 million in individual policies by 1970.

Tax policy increases the demand for employer-based health insurance by making the insurance more attractive relative to wages. When wages are taxed and health insurance is not, employees have an incentive to favor additional health insurance over additional wages. This discount, or tax subsidy, for the purchase of health insurance is directly affected by one's marginal tax rate (MTR), which means that the sub-

**Figure 1 Private Hospital Insurance Coverage: Group
versus Individual, 1940–1970**

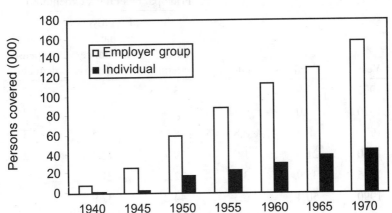

SOURCE: U.S. Bureau of the Census (1975). Employer group is the total
of persons covered by Blue Cross/Blue Shield (B403) plus insurance company group policies (B404).

sidy is greater for higher-income people than for lower-income people.
This also explains why the total amount of the tax subsidy has
increased over time as increases in income have pushed more employees into higher tax brackets. To illustrate, Feldstein and Allison (1991)
found that MTRs for federal taxes in 1969 ranged from 13 percent for
incomes under $1,000 to 36 percent for incomes over $25,000. They
estimated that the total tax subsidy in 1969 was $2 billion, which
implies a 15 percent discount from $15.7 billion total health insurance
premiums in that year. In an update of these estimates, Feldstein found
that the tax subsidy in 1978 exceeded $10 billion on insurance premi-
ums totaling $42 billion, which implies a discount of 24 percent.

Another indication of the growth in the value of the tax subsidy is
the estimates of tax expenditures published by the Congressional Budget Office (1992), which are presented in Table 1. This study estimated
the actual loss in federal and state tax receipts due to the exclusion of
employer-based health insurance from 1969 through 1990 with projections for 1995 and 2000.[3] These estimates show that since 1969, the
value of the medical expense deduction has declined in importance rel-

Table 1 Health Related Tax Expenditures, 1969–2000,[a] ($, billions)

			Principal federal tax expenditures		
Year	Total	State	Total federal	Employer-paid insurance premiums	Medical expense deduction
1969	3.9	0.3	3.6	1.5	1.7
1970	4.0	0.4	3.6	1.5	1.7
1975	8.7	0.8	8.0	3.5	2.3
1980	21.6	1.9	19.7	12.4	3.2
1985	35.9	3.7	32.2	21.7	3.6
1990	50.4	6.3	44.2	32.9	2.8
1995	86.8	9.9	76.8	58.4	4.2
2000	144.0	16.2	127.8	96.3	8.2

SOURCE: Congressional Budget Office (1992).
[a] Untaxed Medicare benefits, deductibility of charitable contributions, and interest on state and local bonds for nonprofit hospitals are not included in these data.

ative to employer-paid health insurance premiums. The table also illustrates the dominance of federal taxes over state taxes, although the MTR of states varies from 0 to 10 percent. This means that some taxpayers in the highest federal tax brackets and in some of the high-tax states may get tax subsidies exceeding 50 percent when they obtain health insurance through their employers. While Sheils and Hogan (1999, p. 179) found that 68.7 percent of tax expenditures in 1998 went to those with incomes of $50,000 or more, their estimate of an average family tax expenditure of $1,031 implies that the average family receives a discount of approximately 2 percent of family income.[4]

Given the size of this tax subsidy and the fact that it could be obtained only by purchasing one's health insurance through one's employer, it is not surprising that it had a strong effect on the structural development of the health insurance industry. The subsidy gave incentives to employees and their unions to seek relatively more increases in health insurance benefits than wages since only the latter were taxed. Policies that covered primarily hospital stays in the 1940s gradually added surgical (major medical) benefits, outpatient physician services, and later coverage for such routine services as dental care and eyeglasses. In addition to the expansion of types of coverage, the degree of coverage also increased, resulting in higher maximum benefits, coverage of dependents, and lower levels of cost sharing (deductibles and co-payments). While such expansions obviously increased both the number of people covered and the extent of their coverage, they also had the usual moral hazard effects of insurance, the tendency of people with insurance to use more of the covered services since they were at least partially shielded from the effects of the cost of the coverage.[5] The result of this tax-induced increase in demand for both health insurance and medical care was an increase in both the quantity and cost of medical care beyond the levels that could have been expected in a less distorted market. Feldstein and Allison (1981, p. 216) concluded their 1972 pioneering study of the effects of the tax treatment of health insurance by concluding that the subsidy "causes a substantial revenue loss, distributes these tax reductions very regressively, encourages an excessive purchase of insurance, distorts the demand for health services, and thus inflates the prices of these services."

If the tax treatment of health insurance helps explain how we developed our present system of health insurance with its built-in incentives for inefficiency, what role, if any, can tax policy play in solving the policy problems we now face? The next section turns to this perplexing issue.

LIVING WITH AN INEFFICIENT HEALTH CARE MARKET: PROSPECTS OF EFFICIENT REFORM

Since economists have been responsible for identifying the distorting effects of tax policy, one would expect that they have also been the ones proposing changes in the tax treatment of health insurance. That has indeed been the case, starting with Feldstein in the early 1970s and proceeding to the present.[6] Except for a brief period when a tax cap proposal was included in President Reagan's 1984 budget submission to the Congress, a serious proposal to substantially reduce the tax subsidy to health insurance has not been proposed by any member of congress.[7]   The politics of such a proposal are not hard to understand given that a relatively large subsidy that has gradually grown in size and importance over the last 57 years has created strong political support for the status quo.[8]   The situation was best captured by Havighurst (1995, p. 102) when he wrote,

> [A] tax subsidy is insidious precisely because, in addition to being an off-budget public expenditure, it can misallocate huge amounts of society's resources, yet be entirely painless at the level of individual producers and consumers. Since the affected interests simply adjust their behavior to the incentives created, they have no occasion to complain or to call for political attention.[9]

But the world is never static, and the existing policy is creating other problems that may be changing the reward structure for politicians. Tax policy, by increasing the demand for health insurance, has increased the cost of both health insurance and medical care. In addition, it has created incentives that have expanded covered benefits and reduced deductibles and co-payments. Although tax policy can be credited with increasing health insurance coverage among the majority of laborers who are in unions and work for larger firms, it has made it more difficult for lower-income workers, the self-employed, and those who are more transitory in their employment arrangements, as well as the dependents of these workers. In addition, Pauly and Berger (1999) have argued that tax policy, by placing the choice of plans and cost-containment strategy in the hands of employers, has increased employees' dissatisfaction with managed care—the so-called managed care backlash.

These somewhat complicated effects of tax policy have exacerbated the main policy problems of cost, lack of coverage, and concerns about quality that are the central issues in today's policy debates. The policy concepts that are being discussed cover a wide range of ideological beliefs about what causes the problem and what policies should be adopted to correct them. The specific proposals from each camp reflect these ideological beliefs. Liberal proposals have traditionally featured some form of federal mandates to assure universal coverage, either mandates for individuals to buy or employers to provide insurance. But the strong opposition to the mandates in the Clinton health proposal has made even the Democrats leery of this approach. Instead, they now lead with expansions of specific government programs such as Medicare for the near-elderly, Medicaid for the low-income, and increased subsidies for safety-net providers treating the indigent. Expansion of the Medicaid eligibility provisions for children established in the State Children's Health Insurance Program (S-CHIP) in the Balanced Budget Act of 1997 is a common feature in President Clinton's and Al Gore's proposals.[10]

Even among Democrats, direct subsidies to individuals or business firms are somewhat out of vogue when they cannot be tied into an existing program such as S-CHIP or traditional Medicaid. While not generally opposed to government administration of a program, they do seem sensitive to the current popular criticism of the ability of federal and state welfare bureaucracies to effectively run such programs. For this reason, some Democrats have turned to tax credits as the most expedient means to provide subsidies to the uninsured.

Refundable tax credits are the principle subsidy mechanism in two separate proposals by long-time Democratic advocates for universal coverage, Congressmen Pete Stark (D., California) and Jim McDermott (D., Washington).[11] These two proposals differ in several respects, but mostly in how they would determine the tax credit. Representative Stark would provide a 100 percent subsidy for the amount paid for qualified health insurance up to a cap of $3,600 for a family of four. It would only be available to those without other forms of coverage. Representative McDermott's tax credit would be 30 percent of the amount paid for health insurance limited by the person's income and Social Security tax liability. Of course, the more generous the tax credit and the more people who are eligible for it, the greater the cost of the program. Because Democrats have been less interested than the Republicans in using federal funds for defense or tax cuts, they have been more willing to propose more expensive tax credit proposals.

Democratic presidential candidates have developed extensive health proposals that include tax credits. Vice President Gore proposed a 25 percent credit that goes to small businesses whose employees choose to get their insurance through a purchasing cooperative. He also proposed a 25 percent refundable tax credit for people who are not covered by their employers and purchase individual insurance.[12] Senator Bill Bradley, in addition to providing full subsidies for health insurance premiums for the low-income, proposed to use income-based refundable tax credits as the means for subsidizing both children and adults.[13]

Republicans have traditionally been less active than Democrats in proposing specific health care plans. They apparently reason that health care is a Democratic issue and that they are better off politically playing a defensive role. But Republicans have been forced by the public's demand for solutions to the growing inequities and other problems in the health care sector to become more active in this field in recent years. Proposals based on Medical Savings Accounts (MSA) and tax credits have been popular with Republicans because they are seen as ways to promote individual choice without expanding bureaucratic control. Specific tax credit proposals have been introduced by three Republicans, Representatives Nancy Johnson (R., Connecticut), Dick Armey (R., Texas), and John Shadegg (R., Arizona). The tax credits in these plans are less generous than Stark's or McDermott's, for example, covering 60 percent of the amount paid for health insurance up to a limit of $2,400 for a family in the Johnson plan and 100 percent of the amount paid up to a $1,000 family cap in the Shadegg plan.[14]

The Republican presidential candidates face a dilemma when it comes to health care. The professional pollsters are telling them that health care is not an important issue among Republicans voters during the primaries, but it will be one of the leading issues in the national elections (Serafini 2000, pp. 336–337). So far, George W. Bush and John McCain have made only general remarks about their approach to health policy and have not come forward with detailed plans similar to the Bradley and Gore plans. Many observers believe that because tax credits were not included in Governor Bush's tax proposals, they have already been rejected in favor of a proposal to provide new block grants to the states for the purpose of expanding coverage to the uninsured. All we know for sure is that his advisers are still working on a plan to be used in the general election.

Senator McCain has mostly talked about new efforts to expand the coverage of children through Medicaid and S-CHIP and the expansion of MSAs and care for veterans (Serafini 2000, p. 337). His Web site even contains a proposal to "use the tax code to provide powerful incentives for employers and individuals to obtain affordable coverage."[15]

As yet, there does not seem to be a detailed proposal based on tax credits.

Because winning the nomination in the primaries is the first order of business for both candidates, it is not surprising that health policy is not at the forefront of their agendas. What is important for our purposes is the position occupied by tax credits in the health policy debate. While both parties have approached health policy from different ideological directions, the most common feature in the serious proposals to reform the health insurance market all involve some variation of a tax credit. Whether tax credits will turn out to be solid grounds for compromise or just another pool of political quicksand has yet to be determined. But there seems to be strong opposition to any set of alternative approaches, be they the expansion of existing programs (Medicare, Medicaid, or MSAs) or new ideas to expand insurance in the individual and small-group markets.

ISSUES IN DESIGNING AN EFFECTIVE TAX CREDIT FOR HEALTH INSURANCE: THE DEVIL IS IN THE DETAILS

If tax credits are to become the basis for a political compromise, a number of key issues will have to be addressed. In the last year a rather large, and in my view overly pessimistic, set of studies about the details of using tax credits to expand health insurance has emerged.[16] Analysis that is more optimistic is in a distinct minority.[17] The following will not try to debunk all the criticism, but will attempt to identify the issues and raise the possibility that we now know enough to give tax credits a try.

The first basic question about tax credits is, will they work? If the objective is to induce low-income working employees to choose to buy health insurance for themselves and their dependents, what kind of subsidy will it take to persuade a significant number to do so? And, is it best to subsidize the small employer, as Vice President Gore proposes to do, or is it best to subsidize individuals, as most of the other proposals do? Does the form of the tax subsidy matter? Are tax credits more effective than tax deductions? Should tax credits be refundable? Should they be a fixed dollar amount or a percentage of the cost of insurance? Is the IRS capable of adding such a scheme to an already complicated tax code? While all of these questions are difficult, it turns out that there is some analysis, and even some empirical research, to give us some answers.

Several elasticity studies have been done about the likely response of employees to tax subsidies to determine the take-up rate.[18] Four of these studies are illustrated by the four demand curves in Figure 2. While not drawn to scale, they represent the order of magnitude of the estimates, ranging from the most inelastic by Chernew, Frick, and McLaughlin (1997) to the most responsive by Pauly and Herring (1999). Based on these elasticity estimates, projections are then made on the likely response of various groups of people to various tax credit plans. The results are difficult to compare because there is not a common definition of a tax credit proposal and because they use different assumptions and data to make their estimates. Still, some useful lessons can be learned by comparing the results of three of the studies, which are illustrated in Figures 3–5.

Sheils, Hogan, and Haught used a price elasticity of –0.203, which, when applied to national numbers, implies a "loss of coverage for about 300,000 persons" for a 1 percent increase in the price of insurance (Sheils, Hogan, and Haught 1999, pp. 56–57). First, Figure 3 illustrates their estimates of what would happen to the number of unin-

Figure 2 Elasticity Estimates

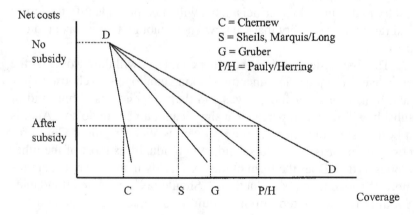

Figure 3 Estimated Tax Subsidy Effects in 2000

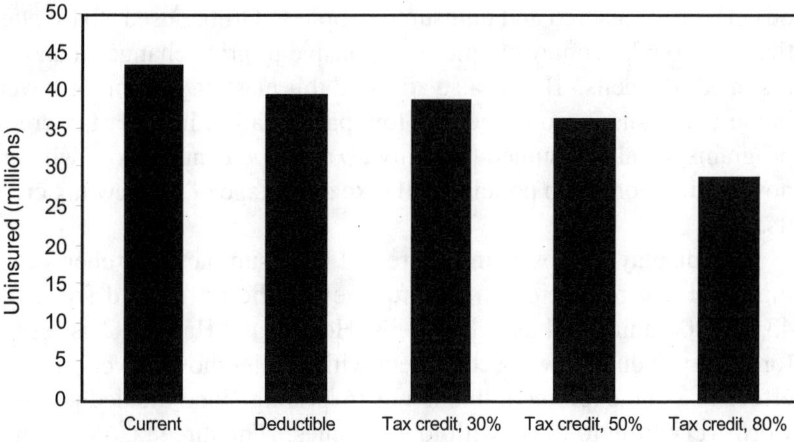

SOURCE: Sheils, Hogan, and Haught (1999).

sured if a tax deduction were given to those without access to employer coverage. The authors then showed the effects of refundable tax credits of 30 percent, 59 percent, and 80 percent made available to all those without access to employer coverage. Their deduction is assumed to be "above the line"; that is, it is subtracted from adjusted gross income so it is available to all taxpayers for nongroup premiums, even those who do not itemize deductions. They found that for the year 2000, 12.2 million of the 51.7 million who would be eligible for the deduction would take the deduction, but that 68 percent of these would be people who were already purchasing nongroup coverage. Their relatively low elasticity assumption (compared to the others below) restrains their estimates of the reduction in the uninsured as the amount of the credit is increased. Meanwhile, the higher levels of tax credits raise the costs to the federal government, from $11.3 billion per year for the 30 percent credit to $50.3 billion for the 80 percent credit. They argue that only by eliminating the present tax exclusion and mandating individual coverage, as is done in the Heritage plan, can universal coverage be achieved at a more reasonable cost to the federal budget. [19]

The next set of estimates are by Jonathan Gruber, who estimated the effects of a tax deduction and different types of tax credits on various classes of insured and uninsured people.[20] Gruber used a base elasticity of –0.625, somewhat more responsive to price changes than that assumed by Sheils. But he also adjusted this elasticity down for lower-income persons.[21] To reflect the low participation in other tax credit programs, he also assumed that only 50 to 90 percent of those who are now buying nongroup policies will take advantage of the new tax credits.

For display purposes, in Figure 4, I have subtracted Gruber's estimates of the reduction in the number of the uninsured from the 43,450,000 uninsured used by Sheils, Hogan, and Haught. His results for the tax deduction were consistent with Sheils, showing very modest effects. As he explained, this is not surprising since the deduction is worth very little to those with low incomes. The three tax credit proposals illustrated in Figure 4 are all refundable but are assumed to apply for only nongroup insurance. But, since all persons are assumed to be eligible, each of these has a strong effect on inducing people with

Figure 4 Estimated Tax Subsidy Effects in 1999[a]

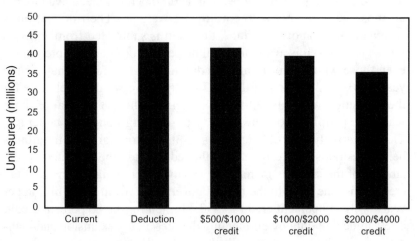

SOURCE: Gruber (2000), Tables 1A, 3A, 6A, and 7A.

[a]These estimates assume the tax credit is refundable and is for nongroup policies only, but that all are eligible.

group insurance to switch to the nongroup market. In the most generous case of a tax credit of $2,000 for an individual and $4,000 for a family, Gruber estimated that almost 14 million people who previously had group insurance would switch to the nongroup market.[22] Although not illustrated in Figure 4, he also finds that this switching out of group policies would be reduced to only four million if the credits were restricted only to those not presently offered health insurance.[23]

Pauly and Herring (1999) concentrated their analysis on the 32.3 million workers and their dependents who are uninsured, the part of the population that tax credits are primarily designed to reach. They argued that their estimates are substantially different from other estimates because the elasticities used by Gruber, Sheils, and others have been obtained from studies of other working populations that are predominantly higher income than the low-income population tax credits are designed to help (Pauly and Herring 1999, p. 2 and p. 14).[24] As illustrated in Figure 5, they provide separate estimates of three levels of tax credits showing the results separately for those below and above 300 percent of the federal poverty level. No restrictions or caps are placed on eligibility for the credits.

Figure 5 Effects of Tax Credits on the Uninsured

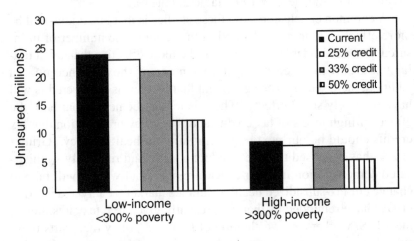

SOURCE: Pauly and Herring (1999).

Pauly and Herring (1999) drew several conclusions from their estimates, most of which can be seen in Figure 5. First, refundable tax
credits are going to be more effective on the low-income than on
higher-income because they are, by design, targeted more toward low-
income people. A given percentage credit will have a stronger effect
on the low-income compared to higher-income because it will move
more of them over their "reservation price" and give them a reason to
make a decision different from the one they had made without the subsidy. But, low levels of subsidy will not be as effective at higher
incomes because most people who have already made a decision not to
buy insurance will not be induced to change their minds until they see a
substantial difference in their cost of insurance. Pauly and Herring
reached the same conclusion as Sheils and Gruber—that small tax
credits are not likely to have a large effect on the number of the uninsured. But unlike the previous studies, they found that higher levels of
subsidy could have substantial effects on the uninsured, especially the
low-income uninsured. Assuming a 40 percent loading factor, their 50
percent tax credit reduces the uninsured by 45 percent; if a larger individual insurance market would reduce loading factors to 30 percent,
they estimate that the number of uninsured would decrease by 80.5 percent (Pauly and Herring 1999, table 2).[25] They also estimated that a tax
credit equal to two-thirds of the premium would reduce the uninsured
to zero (Pauly and Herring 1999, table 2, note c).

A common conclusion from these studies is that tax credits will be
more effective than a tax deduction in reducing the number of uninsured, and a refundable tax credit will be more effective than a flat dollar tax credit in reaching relatively more of the low-income. In
addition, there seems to be agreement that low levels of tax credits will
have relatively small effects. There is less agreement about both the
effects of high levels of tax credits and the policy prescription that tax
credits should be our next major initiative in health policy. Gruber
(1999) has proposed that we conduct a large and relatively sophisti-
cated demonstration in order to learn more about what it will take to
change our tax-subsidized health insurance market. Pauly and Herring
(1999) have reminded us that we presently give large tax subsidies to
most U.S. workers, so we should not look at a policy that shifts these
subsidies as necessarily a net loss in economic efficiency. A policy that
both increases government expenditures and decreases government

revenue may have distributional effects without imposing a real economic loss (Pauly and Herring 1999, p. 3 and p. 27).

PROSPECTS FOR THE FUTURE: POSITIVE ECONOMICS AND DISMAL POLITICS

To paraphrase one of the oldest jokes about economists, we have now lined up end-to-end all the economists working on tax credits and they can't reach a conclusion. So, one might ask, if the economists can not agree, how would we ever expect politicians to agree? The answer is that tax credits might become the basis for a political compromise to expand health insurance coverage if enough politicians believe that there is no chance to get the alternative policies they prefer. The next election of the president and the congress will have a big influence on that possibility.

Without having a comparative advantage in making political predictions, let us look at three possible outcomes. The first is that the Republicans win both the White House and the House of Representatives (the Senate is assumed to remain in the hands of the Republicans in all three cases). This result will likely bring about less overall interest in health policy, and certainly not much interest in achieving universal coverage. There will be some interest in expanding the use of MSAs, health marts, and block grants to states, but there will not likely be enough agreement on premium support to do much about Medicare. The Republicans are likely to try to pass some low-cost, income-based prescription drug benefit for Medicare. Their interest in cutting taxes and controlling the growth in federal expenditures will not leave much room for expensive new health programs like tax credits.

The second outcome to consider is that the Democrats win both the White House and the House of Representatives. Even without control of the Senate, they will be in a position to carry out a substantial part of their agenda, including expansions of S-CHIP to families of uninsured children, higher income eligibility for Medicaid, and more direct subsidies to safety-net providers. More likely too would be an expansive Medicare drug benefit and a patient protection act with a strong right to sue. Expanding insurance coverage in the private sector through complicated and expensive tax credits are not likely to be very popular.

The third possibility is, of course, that party control is split between the White House and the House of Representatives. Regardless of how this happens, and assuming that one party does not gain the power to overcome a veto, it leaves us in somewhat of a political stalemate, not unlike the situation we have mostly been in for the last 20 years. In such a situation, neither party has the ability to carry out its preferred agenda. Tax credits, which already enjoy some bipartisan support, might emerge as the basis for action, but only if there is a strong desire to do something about private coverage. Two current trends, if continued, could help bring that about. If the cost of health care and health insurance premiums continue to increase, this could increase the number of the uninsured as some employers drop coverage and others cut back on the proportion of the premium that they cover, causing more employees to decline coverage for themselves and/or their dependents. In addition, if more firms decide to convert to a defined contribution approach, this could improve the efficiency of the individual market, making the cost-effectiveness of a tax credit approach more acceptable to the Congress.[26]

That is anything but a definitive prediction, but I have lived in Washington too long to have much faith in anyone's ability to predict the future of political events. If politicians decide that tax credits are the only way to achieve a desired political objective, then there is enough positive economic analysis around to tell them how to make them work. If they were accompanied with some limit on the tax exclusion, we could make a faster start on the road back to a more efficient health care market. Politics at this time is too dismal for that much change.

Notes

1. This section draws heavily on Helms (1999).
2. This history is discussed in more detail in Helms (1999), pp. 9–12.
3. Sheils and Hogan (1999) provide later estimates of tax expenditures for 1998 that seem consistent with the Congressional Budget Office projections. For 1998, they estimated state tax expenditures of $13.6 billion and federal tax expenditures of $111.2 billion.

4. Computed by dividing the average family tax expenditure by average family income of $51,855, the latter coming from U.S. Census Bureau, "Historical Income Tables: Experimental Measures," Table RDI-1, http://www.census.gov/hhes/income/histinc/rdi01.html.

5. For readable explanations of the basic economics of insurance, see Hall (1994), especially Chapter 2, and Pauly (1980), pp. 201–219.

6. For examples of proposals placing emphasis on capping or eliminating the tax exclusion, see Feldstein (1971); Pauly et al. (1992); Butler (1992); Steuerle (1993); and Arnett (1999).

7. The Administration's proposal was sent to Congress on February 28, 1993, and introduced as, "The Health Care Cost Containment Tax Act of 1983," S.640.

8. For one defense of the present system, see Custer, Kahn, and Wildsmith (1999).

9. Havighurst also says, ". . . capping the tax subsidy is a notion that only a policy wonk could love, a meritorious policy idea with no natural political constituency," p. 103.

10. One-third of the 25 million low-income uninsured are children (Kaiser Commission on Medicaid and the Uninsured 1999).

11. A more complete description of these and other current tax-related proposals can be found in Weiss and Garay (2000).

12. Http://www.algore2000.com/agenda/agenda_healthcare.html, pp. 3–4. Accessed February 2000.

13. Http://www.billbradley.com/bin/article.pl?path=280999/3.   Accessed February 2000.

14. The Armey plan covers 100 percent of the amount paid up to a cap of $3,000 for a family of four (Weiss and Garay 2000, p. 8).

15. See Health Care, p. 10, at http://63.224.30.9/issues/qna.html.

16. For examples of this literature, each of which contains useful analysis and data, see Blumberg (1999); Meyer, Silow-Carroll, and Wicks (2000); Gruber and Levitt (2000); and Salisbury (1999).

17. For more positive views of tax credits, see Steuerle (1993); Pauly et al. (1992); Butler (1992); Pauly (1999); and Butler and Kendall (1999).

18. Chernew, Frick, and McLaughlin (1997); Sheils, Hogan, and Haught (1999); Gruber and Levitt (2000); and Pauly and Herring (1999).

19. Sheils, Hogan, and Haught (1999), executive summary-1.

20. These estimates are summarized in Gruber and Levitt (2000), but the information here is taken from Gruber's (2000) technical report.

21. Gruber (2000), p. 38.

22. Gruber (2000), table 7A.

23. Gruber (2000), table 4A.

24. Pauly and Herring (1999) also make estimates assuming a 30 percent loading factor in the nongroup market, but only the more restrictive 40 percent assumption is shown in Figure 4.

25. For a discussion of how an expanded individual market could lower loading factors and improve the risk pooling function of insurance, see Pauly, Percy, and Herring (1999).
26. For a recent account of the interest in a defined contribution approach, see Winslow and Gentry (2000).

References

Arnett, Grace-Marie. 1999. *Empowering Health Care Consumers through Tax Reform.* Ann Arbor, Michigan: University of Michigan Press.

Blumberg, Linda J. 1999. *Expanding Health Insurance Coverage: Are Tax Credits the Right Track to Take?* Washington, D.C.: The Urban Institute.

Butler, Stuart M. 1992. *A Policy Maker's Guide to the Health Care Crisis, Part II: The Heritage Foundation Consumer Choice Health Plan.* Washington, D.C.: Heritage Foundation.

Butler, Stuart, and David B. Kendall. 1999. "Expanding Access and Choice for Health Care Consumers through Tax Reform." *Health Affairs* 18(6): 45–57.

Chernew, Michael E., K. Frick, and Catherine G. McLaughlin. 1997. "The Demand for Health Insurance by Low-Income Workers: Can Reduced Premiums Achieve Full Coverage?" *Health Services Research* 32(4): 453–470.

Congressional Budget Office. 1992. *Projections of National Health Expenditures*, October, p. 56.

Custer, William S., Charles N. Kahn III, and Thomas F. Wildsmith IV. 1999. "Why We Should Keep the Employment-Based Health Insurance System." *Health Affairs* 18(6): 115–123.

Feldstein, Martin. 1971. "A New Approach to National Health Insurance." *The Public Interest 23*(Spring): 93–105.

Feldstein, Martin, and Elisabeth Allison. 1981. "Tax Subsidies of Private Health Insurance: Distribution, Revenue Loss, and Effects." In *Hospital Costs and Health Insurance*, Martin Feldstein, ed. Cambridge, Massachusetts: Harvard University Press, Table 7.2

Field, Marilyn J., and Harold T. Shapiro, eds. 1993. *Employment and Health Benefits: A Connection at Risk,* Washington, D.C.: National Academy Press, p. 70.

Glied, Sherry. 1994. *Revising the Tax Treatment of Employer-Provided Health Insurance,* Washington, D.C.: AEI Press, p. 5.

Gruber, Jonathan. 1999. "Tax Subsidies for Health Insurance: What Do We Need to Know, What We Do Know, and How We Could Learn More." Draft paper prepared for the Robert Woods Johnson Foundation Conference "Tax Credits as a Mechanism for Expanding Health Care Coverage," held in Washington, D.C., December 16.

_____. 2000. "Tax Subsidies for Health Insurance: Evaluating the Costs and Benefits." Technical report prepared for the Kaiser Family Foundation, January. Available on the Internet at http://kff.org/content/2000/01101999a/gruber.pdf. Accessed February 2000.

Gruber, Jonathan, and Larry Levitt. 2000. "Tax Subsidies for Health Insurance: Costs and Benefits." *Health Affairs* 19(1): 72–85.

Hall, Mark A. 1994. *Reforming Private Health Insurance.* Washington, D.C.: AEI Press.

Havighurst, Clark C. 1995. *Health Care Choices.* Washington, D.C.: AEI Press.

Helms, Robert B. 1999. "The Tax Treatment of Health Insurance: Early History and Evidence, 1940–1970." In *Empowering Health Care Consumers through Tax Reform,* Grace-Marie Arnett, ed. Ann Arbor: The University of Michigan Press, pp. 9–12.

Kaiser Commission on Medicaid and the Uninsured. 1999. "A Profile of the Low-Income Uninsured." Washington, D.C.: Kaiser Family Foundation. Available on the Internet at http://kff.org/content/1999/2158/lowincome-unins.pdf. Accessed January 2001.

Meyer, Jack A., Sharon Silow-Carroll, and Elliot K. Wicks. 2000. *Tax Reform to Expand Health Coverage: Administrative Issues and Challenges.* Washington, D.C.: Kaiser Family Foundation, January.

Pauly, Mark V. 1980. "Overinsurance: The Conceptual Issues." In *National Health Insurance: What Now, What Later, What Never?,* Mark V. Pauly, ed. Washington, D.C.: AEI Press.

_____. 1999. *Extending Health Insurance through Tax Credits.* Washington, D.C.: Kaiser Family Foundation.

Pauly, Mark V., and Marc L. Berger. 1999. "Why Should Managed Care be Regulated?" In *Regulating Managed Care: Theory, Practice, and Future Options,* Stuart Altman, Uwe E. Reinhardt, and David Shactman, eds. San Francisco: Jossey-Bass, pp. 53–74.

Pauly, Mark, and Brad Herring. 1999. "Cutting Taxes for Insuring: Options and Effects of Tax Credits for Health Insurance." Paper presented at conference sponsored by the Council on the Economic Impact of Health System Change, held in Washington, D.C., December.

Pauly, Mark, Allison Percy, and Bradley Herring. 1999. "Individual versus Job-Based Health Insurance: Weighing the Pros and Cons." *Health Affairs* 18(6): 28–44.

Pauly, Mark V., Patricia Danzon, Paul Feldstein, and John S. Hoff. 1992. *Responsible National Health Insurance.* Washington, D.C.: The AEI Press.

Salisbury, Dallas, ed. 1999. *Severing the Link between Health Insurance and Employment.* Washington, D.C.: Employee Benefit Research Institute.

Serafini, Marilyn Werber. 2000. "McCain's Cure—Health Care Has So Far Been Mostly Ignored by the GOP Presidential Contenders. Except for McCain." *National Journal* 32(5): 336–337.

Sheils, John, and Paul Hogan. 1999. "Cost of Tax-Exempt Health Benefits in 1998." *Health Affairs* 18(2): 178.

Sheils, John, Paul Hogan, and Randall Haught. 1999. *Health Insurance and Taxes: The Impact of Proposed Changes in Current Federal Policy.* Washington, D.C.: The National Coalition on Health Care.

Somers, Herman M., and Anna R. Somers. 1961. *Doctors, Patients, and Health Insurance.* Washington, D.C.: The Brookings Institution.

Steuerle, C. Eugene. 1993. "The Search for Adaptable Health Policy through Finance-Based Reform." In *American Health Policy: Critical Issues for Reform,* Robert B. Helms, ed. Washington, D.C.: AEI Press, pp. 346–351.

U.S. Bureau of the Census. 1975. *Historical Statistics of the United States, Colonial Times to 1970, Part 1.* Washington, D.C.: U.S. Department of Commerce.

_____. 1990. *Statistical Abstract of the United States: 1990.* Washington, D.C.: U.S. Department of Commerce, Table 695.

Weiss, Randall, and Mark Garay. 2000. *Recent Tax Proposals to Increase Health Insurance Coverage.* Washington, D.C.: The Kaiser Family Foundation.

White, William D. 1982. "The American Hospital Industry Since 1900: A Short History." In *Advances in Health Economics and Health Services Research,* Vol. 3, Richard M. Scheffler and Louis F. Rossiter, eds. Greenwich, Connecticut: JAI Press Inc., p. 162.

Winslow, Ron, and Carol Gentry. 2000. "Companies Consider Letting Employees Handle Their Health Benefits Decisions." *The Wall Street Journal,* February 8.

CITED AUTHOR INDEX

The italic letters *f*, *n*, or *t* following a page number indicate that the cited name is in a figure, note, or table, respectively, on that page.

SUBJECT INDEX

The italic letters *f, n* or *t* following a page number indicate that the subject information is in a figure, note, or a table, respectively, on that page.

About the Institute

The W.E. Upjohn Institute for Employment Research is a nonprofit research organization devoted to finding and promoting solutions to employment-related problems at the national, state, and local levels. It is an activity of the W.E. Upjohn Unemployment Trustee Corporation, which was established in 1932 to administer a fund set aside by the late Dr. W.E. Upjohn, founder of The Upjohn Company, to seek ways to counteract the loss of employment income during economic downturns.

The Institute is funded largely by income from the W.E. Upjohn Unemployment Trust, supplemented by outside grants, contracts, and sales of publications. Activities of the Institute comprise the following elements: 1) a research program conducted by a resident staff of professional social scientists; 2) a competitive grant program, which expands and complements the internal research program by providing financial support to researchers outside the Institute; 3) a publications program, which provides the major vehicle for disseminating the research of staff and grantees, as well as other selected works in the field; and 4) an Employment Management Services division, which manages most of the publicly funded employment and training programs in the local area.

The broad objectives of the Institute's research, grant, and publication programs are to 1) promote scholarship and experimentation on issues of public and private employment and unemployment policy, and 2) make knowledge and scholarship relevant and useful to policymakers in their pursuit of solutions to employment and unemployment problems.

Current areas of concentration for these programs include causes, consequences, and measures to alleviate unemployment; social insurance and income maintenance programs; compensation; workforce quality; work arrangements; family labor issues; labor-management relations; and regional economic development and local labor markets.

163